Treasures
of Ancient
EGYPT

Treasures
of Ancient
EGYPT

Discover the Masterpieces
of the Pharaohs

General Editor: Catherine Chambers

amber
BOOKS

First published in 2007 by
Amber Books Ltd
Bradley's Close
74–77 White Lion Street
London N1 9PF
United Kingdom
www.amberbooks.co.uk

Distributed in the UK by
Bookmart Ltd
Blaby Road
Wigston
Leicester
LE18 4SE

ISBN 978-1-905704-51-4

This material was originally published in partwork form as *The Glory of Ancient Egypt*

Picture Credits
All images courtesy of DeAgostini UK Ltd except:
6: NASA, 40: Werner Forman Archive/Fitzwilliam Museum,
72: Werner Forman Archive, 94: Corbis (Gianni Dagli Orti),
124: Topfoto (The British Museum/HIP),
148: Corbis (Charles & Josette Lenar)

Printed and bound in Dubai

10 9 8 7 6 5 4 3 2 1

Contents

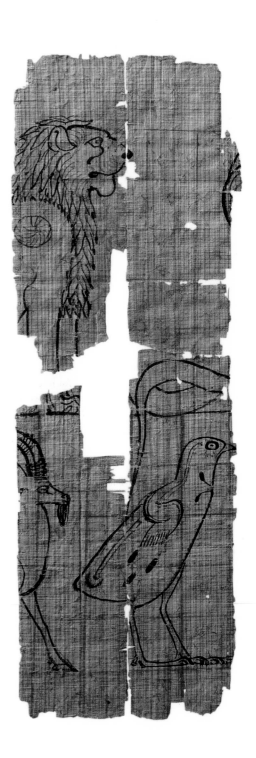

Introduction

Egypt extends from the sweltering heart of the Sahara in the south to the Mediterranean to the north. As such, her geographic profile seems quite unpromising in terms of serving human development. Yet in this setting, ancient Egypt emerged as a dynamic, innovative and creative civilization that lasted over 3,000 years. She could have achieved none of this, however, without one crucial factor – the mighty River Nile, which runs like a twisting, nerve-filled spine along her back.

In this setting, the treasures of Ancient Egypt were the product of an organized society that enjoyed long-term economic success. But this order had come out of the chaos of a climatic change that probably began in around 8000 B.C.E. when the once-cooler savannah grasslands warmed up and dried out, creating the expansive Sahara. From then on, Nomadic hunter-gatherers responded to the desertification of their pastures by retreating to the damper, more fertile Nile Valley.

This was the perfect stimulus for domesticating livestock, developing arable farming, and setting up permanent settlements. The switch to sustainable agriculture in turn started a revolution in tool-making and experimentation with the abundance of local raw materials. It precipitated trading systems, and storage methods to manage agricultural surpluses. Ceramic and stoneware vessels and furnishings soon became valued for their form as well as their function.

By about 4000 B.C.E. a sophisticated material culture was fast developing in the burgeoning towns. A new class of rulers and rich merchants commissioned luxury goods and works of art, and gave thanks for their good fortune by honouring the gods with pious statues and temples.

The Nile from Space
This satellite image clearly shows the strip of cultivated land either side of the winding river Nile, giving way to parched desert beyond.

Why Egypt?
Time, Materials and Methods

Ancient Egypt's treasures are extraordinary in their visual and textural range. But how, in Egypt's breathtaking but apparently hostile landscape, did such a lavish material culture emerge and sustain itself? The secret lies partly in the character of the River Nile. Almost every year it cascaded from its upper reaches in present-day Tanzania, down into the Nile Valley and through the Delta to the Mediterranean. This inundation lasted from about June through to September. Then it would subside, leaving behind a thick layer of dark, wet, fertile sediment. By about November, farmers were able to sow their seeds and plant their crops – relying for a while on the soil's dampness to water the seedlings, then, after it had dried out, on sophisticated water channels and irrigation systems.

Waiting for the flood, farmers and labourers had spare time on their hands – time to manufacture goods, build homes, temples and great tombs, and to be creative. Some became master craftsmen: goldsmiths and coppersmiths, weavers and basketmakers, sculptors of statues and stelae.

The River Nile was also the source of a wide variety of raw materials: clay for bricks and vessels; papyrus for early boat-building, sail-making, and the world's first-known paper. Moreover, the river was a conduit for procuring other raw materials from far-off lands: gold from Nubia, cedar and other aromatic woods from Lebanon, obsidian from more southerly parts of the continent – possibly Ethiopia – and from even further south, ebony, ivory, incense and skins.

Above the waters
To protect themselves from the Nile's annual flood, the Ancient Egyptians traditionally built their towns and villages on high ground, out of the water's reach. Despite these precautions, however, they were not always safe from exceptionally high rises in water level, which could have devastating results.

Art in Ancient Egypt

The artistic mastery of the sculpture, architecture, relief carving and painting of the Ancient Egyptians has captivated mankind throughout the ages.

The art of Ancient Egypt is the record of a culture that remained basically the same over some 3,000 years, although styles did change through the different eras. The stonemasons had mastered working in even the hardest stone from very early on, and large stone obelisks and statues made from diorite, quarzite or limestone have decorated temples since the Old Kingdom (2686–2181 BC).

The sophistication of the craftsmen can be seen in the techniques of quarrying. A single, uncracked block had to be cut from rock and often transported hundreds of kilometres to be worked on further. Large teams of craftsmen created the decorations on graves and temples, with draughtsmen, sculptors and painters collaborating to produce works of art. There are very few cases where a work is signed by a single artist.

▶ **Relief work**
The Egyptians decorated temple and tomb walls with two kinds of carving: sunken reliefs, such as in the temple of Sety I (1294–1279 BC) in Abydos, were cut out of the flat wall, while others were raised, with the surrounding stone being cut away.

▶ **Tombs**
The pharaohs spared no expense in the construction of their 'houses of eternity', the most spectacular examples being the great pyramids of Giza. It has never been fully established how the builders and masons managed to make such perfect constructions.

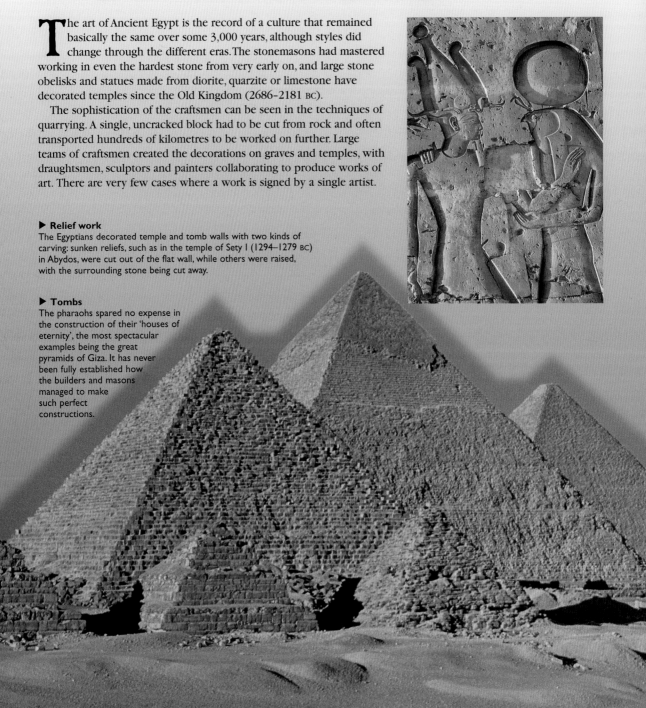

▲ Temples
Countless shrines dedicated to the glory of the gods were built. The most important place of worship, however, was the temple of Amun at Karnak, bordering the Nile, which grew into a large complex of buildings over a period of some 2,000 years.

▲ Painting
In glowing colours that contrasted with the dull tones of the desert landscape, wall paintings depicted scenes of everyday life and religious images. This one, found in the tomb of Horemheb (1323–1295 BC) in the Valley of the Kings, shows gods and the pharaohs in the afterlife.

▶ Sculpture
Stone statues were a form of substitute body for the soul in its life in eternity. The Egyptian artists sought to reflect this idea of timeless existence in their works. In this group, Rameses II (1279–1313 BC) sits between the goddess Mut and the god Amun.

Painters and Paintings

From the Old Kingdom (2686–2181 BC), the art of painting developed in Egypt. Its function was to reflect and perpetuate life and, as such, it was used in tombs and temples for wall decorations and to enhance the sculpture of a relief.

Egyptian art was primarily concerned with ensuring the continuity of life and the universe, and the paintings on the walls of temples and tombs are an idealized reflection of this. The artists did not choose the designs to go on religious monuments. The tomb owners, and the priests or pharaohs of the temples, determined the decorative elements, which generally consisted of faithful but formulaic reproductions of funerary rites, divine cults, myths or historical events.

The slightest failure on the part of the artist in depicting these rituals could threaten the future life of the deceased, or the smooth continuation of the cosmic balance. Scenes from everyday life were also included on wall paintings, however, and here draughtsmen and painters were able to be more uninhibited and lively.

A layer of plaster or stucco *about 3cm (1⅛in) thick provided the surface for the painting. It was wiped and polished to make it as smooth as possible.*

Designs and paints *were applied directly to the dry wall.*

▶ **Step-by-step painting**
Artists worked in teams, with a master craftsman overseeing a number of apprentices. The artists began by covering the wall with a grid, enabling them to copy faithfully from a design drawn up on papyrus. They then traced the outline of the figures in red paint, while their team leader corrected mistakes with black paint. Finally, the painters mixed the powdered pigments with water and an adhesive (acacia gum or egg white). This paint was called 'tempera', and was applied as a flat wash.

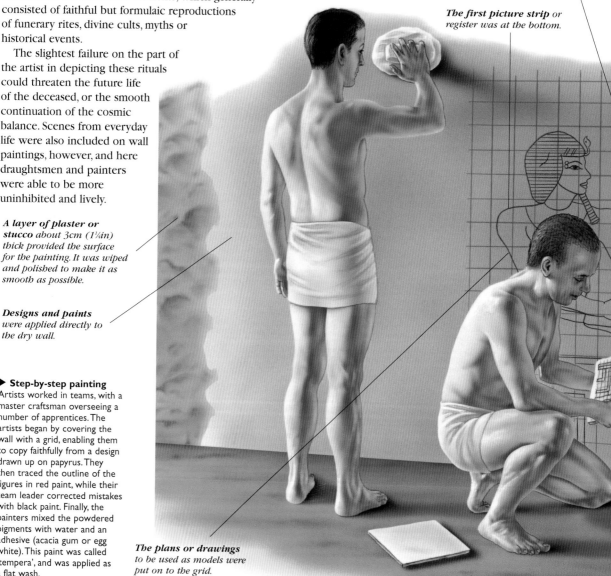

Cords soaked in red paint *marked out the grid on the walls.*

The first picture strip *or register was at the bottom.*

The plans or drawings *to be used as models were put on to the grid.*

Applying the design

To place the design on the wall grid, the draughtsman calculated the number of squares occupied by the figures on the papyrus plan. He then copied them on to the wall, drawing them in the same number of squares so that the proportions were exactly the same.

▼ Artists' equipment
The painters used brushes of different sizes made of plant fibres. They ground the pigments in a stone mortar and mixed them in terra-cotta pots. The sculptors made their incisions by tapping bronze scissors with a wooden mallet.

▼ Paint pigments
The luminous, fresh colours of Egyptian paintings are due to their pigments. Mainly of mineral origin, they were not altered by light. Thus, white has a lime and gypsum base, green came from copper, yellow from ochre, red from iron oxide and blue from azurite.

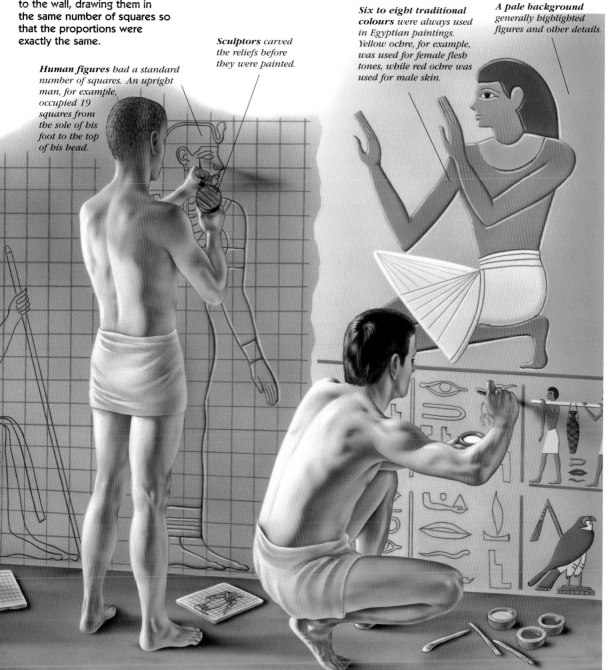

Six to eight traditional colours were always used in Egyptian paintings. Yellow ochre, for example, was used for female flesh tones, while red ochre was used for male skin.

A pale background generally highlighted figures and other details.

Sculptors carved the reliefs before they were painted.

Human figures had a standard number of squares. An upright man, for example, occupied 19 squares from the sole of his foot to the top of his head.

Relief-carving Techniques

Sculpting a relief is much more complicated than painting. For the Egyptians, reliefs were eternal, and were widely used in temples, stelae and in the tombs of high officials, as well as on sarcophagi and other pieces of funerary equipment.

Relief design first appeared in the Predynastic period (5500–3100 BC) on small objects such as cosmetic palettes. It was developed from drawing, from which it took the convention of combining different viewpoints – face-on and from the side – in the same image. From the beginning, relief carvings were usually painted, and only the most important elements of a scene were sculpted in relief. Details, such as wayside plants, woven basket designs or patterned borders on dresses, were added when the stonework was painted to make the picture more vivid.

There are two main types of relief carving. In raised relief, sculptors cut away the material on the outside of a design, leaving it standing proud. In sunken relief, or intaglio, the design is cut into the surface of the stone. The intaglio method was mostly used on outside walls, exploiting light and shade to mould the designs.

▼ **Preparing the walls**
Before relief scenes could be sketched out, the dressed-stone walls were smoothed and polished, and any cracks and holes filled with limestone mortar. A thin coating of plaster was applied to the walls to make it easier to sketch the designs before carving began.

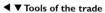

◄ ▼ Tools of the trade
Egyptian sculptors used massive wooden mallets with flat or pointed copper or bronze chisels to carve limestone blocks. Lengths of string soaked in red pigment and stretched between two sticks were used to mark out the design grid on the walls.

The wedjat eye (eye of Horus) is carved in raised relief so that it literally stands out from the design.

Zigzag lines cut into the stone create a simple, repetitive pattern as a decorative motif.

◄ Kawit's sarcophagus
The walls of the tombs of the queens of the Middle Kingdom (2055–1650 BC) were not decorated, but their limestone sarcophagi, such as that of Queen Kawit (c. 2055–2004 BC), bore decorative relief carvings in the palace-façade style.

▼ From sketch to relief
The incomplete tomb of Horemheb (1323–1295 BC) in the Valley of the Kings shows the various stages in the creation of a relief. The wall was covered with a red grid, which helped transfer a papyrus sketch to a larger area. The scene was first sketched in red, then accurately finished in black paint as a final guide for the sculptor. After the relief was carved, the wall was whitewashed and repainted in different colours.

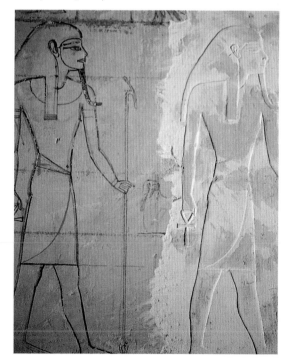

INSIGHT

High and low relief

Throughout the long history of relief carving in Egypt, sculptors worked in what are known technically as bas- (low) relief and haut- (high) relief. Low relief, in which figures and inscriptions are slightly raised against a background that has been chiselled away, was the preferred method. High relief, in which the figures stand out more, and in some cases are almost free-standing statues, is relatively rare, as it involved a great deal more work in cutting away the stone. It did, however, give the carver much more scope for telling detail.

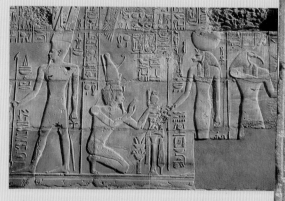

▲ A kneeling king makes an offering to Sekhmet in this low relief from the temple of Amun at Karnak. It dates from the reign of Sety I (1294–1279 BC), a golden age for Egyptian art, and its quality is evident in the fineness of the details.

▼ The Greco-Roman temple of Kom Ombo, dedicated to the crocodile god Sobek and Haroeris, an aspect of Horus, is decorated with reliefs that were mostly made in the first century BC. This carving of a king, with an offering of four sacred vases, shows how high relief can add depth and expression to a face.

▲ The high-relief figures on this stele, which stand proud from the background and are modelled in three dimensions like statues, represent Bak, a sculptor who was in the employ of Akhenaten (1352–1336 BC), and his wife.

Contrasting styles

Depictions in high relief of four protective goddesses – Isis, Nephthys, Serket and Neith – guard the corners of the sarcophagus of Tutankhamun (1336–1327 BC). The hieroglyphs and wedjat eye are rendered in intaglio, and the contrast throws the high-relief figure of Nephthys into much sharper focus.

The goddess Nephthys uses her outstretched arms and wings to protect one corner of the sarcophagus. She wears a large collar with several strings of beads and painted armlets and bracelets.

The eye of Horus, or wedjat eye, and other inscriptions were rendered in intaglio, using a pointed chisel of hardened bronze. The wedjat eye not only protected the mummy, but also allowed it to view the earthly world left behind.

Sculptors of religious scenes, created in order to maintain the cosmic order in temples and assure eternal life for the dead, were not allowed to give free reign to their imaginations, but had to adhere strictly to designs already set out on papyrus; a grid system was used to transfer these to the walls. The carvers had more freedom in rendering scenes of everyday life, and such reliefs are often filled with flashes of humour and well-observed details.

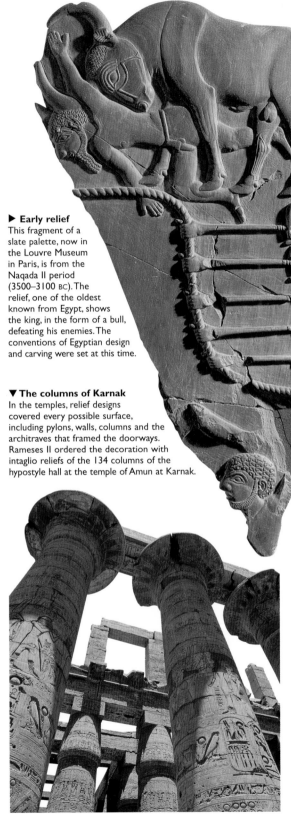

▶ Early relief
This fragment of a slate palette, now in the Louvre Museum in Paris, is from the Naqada II period (3500–3100 BC). The relief, one of the oldest known from Egypt, shows the king, in the form of a bull, defeating his enemies. The conventions of Egyptian design and carving were set at this time.

▲ Added colour
When low reliefs were finished, the walls were covered with a thin layer of stucco and painted in vivid colours, most of which have faded and disappeared over time.

▼ High-relief massacre
This well-modelled relief on the pylon – ceremonial gateway – of the temple complex of Medinet Habu, across the Nile from Luxor, shows Rameses III smiting his enemies.

▼ The columns of Karnak
In the temples, relief designs covered every possible surface, including pylons, walls, columns and the architraves that framed the doorways. Rameses II ordered the decoration with intaglio reliefs of the 134 columns of the hypostyle hall at the temple of Amun at Karnak.

INSIGHT

Intaglio reliefs

Intaglio, the technique of incising an image into stone or other hard materials, was used to illuminate sculptures on the exterior of Egyptian monuments, and on interior sculptures to highlight figures or scenes. Reliefs of this kind were particularly common during the reign of Rameses II.

▲ On Tutankhamun's Canopic shrine, the figures of Nephthys and the Canopic deity Hapy are cut in intaglio on the gilded wood.

▼ Delineation of the images in this intaglio relief of Rameses II in the temple of Luxor would have been more pronounced when painted.

▲ This deeply incised image of Horus is on one of the pylons of Isis's temple at Philae, and shows the effectiveness of the intaglio technique in modelling with light and shade.

Goldsmiths and Jewellers

As early as 5000 BC, necklaces and belts were made along the Nile from beads, plant seeds and various polished stones. From about 4000 BC onwards, the Ancient Egyptians began to use gold, silver and copper to make jewellery.

In Ancient Egypt, both men and women adorned themselves with jewellery, not only as decoration, but also in the form of protective amulets. Virtually every form of jewellery has been recorded, including finger rings, anklets, armlets, girdles and pectorals, necklaces, torques, chokers, diadems, ear studs, earrings and hair ornaments.

Coloured semi-precious stones, such as cornelian, turquoise, feldspar, green and red jasper, amethyst, quartz, agate and lapis lazuli – imported from Afghanistan – were the most commonly used stones. Often, however, they were imitated by coloured glass and faience. Many of the stones were mined in the desert areas of Egypt and in Sinai.

Gold and copper mines were mainly found in the outlying areas of Egypt and Nubia, but during the New Kingdom (1550–1069 BC), much gold was received as

▶ **High-quality gold jewellery**
Objects made from precious metals and precious stones were worn by the nobility in everyday life and used as tomb offerings. The jewellery from the tomb of Tutankhamun (1336–1327 BC) and this gold mask of Psusennes I (1039–991 BC) are of the finest quality.

The eyes and eyebrows, made of lapis lazuli and glass, are set into the thin gold plate of the mask.

The goldsmiths designed the shoulders of the mask as a wide garland of flowers, the so-called wesekh *collar.*

INSIGHT

Nub – precious metal from the mines of Nubia

In Egypt itself, gold was found in Wadi Hammamat (between Qena and the Red Sea); however, when the pharaohs conquered Nubia, they suddenly controlled a rich source of the precious metal. The Ancient Egyptian word for gold, *nub*, even gave its name to this part of the country south of Aswan.

Expeditions to the gold mines, which lay far away from the Nile, had to be carefully planned. Bedouins, who knew not only the exact location of the mines, but also all the water sources along the way, were hired as guides. Small mounds, called alamats (below), were built as signposts for the routes through the desert.

▲ **Falcon pectoral**
The wings of this golden falcon with the head of a ram are inlaid with lapis lazuli, cornelian and turquoise. This pectoral was a tomb offering in the Serapeum of Saqqara.

The golden uraeus serpent was forged separately and attached above the forehead with fine pins.

The cross stripes of the king's headdress, the nemes, were created by engraving the gold plate.

The making of gold jewellery

1. Weighing the gold

2. Smelting the gold in a furnace

3. Hammering and beating the metal into shape

4. Displaying the finished piece

tribute from conquered territories. Egyptian gold was often mixed with a high percentage of silver. This light, or 'white' gold, also called electrum, could be worked at slightly lower temperatures than pure, high-carat gold.

In the Old Kingdom (2686–2181 BC), jewellery-making was a popular theme in tomb decorations. Reliefs show the goldsmithing process, as well as the piercing of pearls and the stringing of necklaces. As craftsmen of the pharaoh, and as makers of protective amulets, jewellers and goldsmiths were held in high esteem.

Textile Production

Tomb paintings and models, as well as surviving pieces of cloth, tell us all about Egyptian clothmaking, from the preparation of fibres through spinning yarn to weaving and dyeing textiles.

L inen, from the fibres of the flax plant, *Linum usitatissimum*, was the principal cloth used in Ancient Egypt. Flax was not a native plant – it came from the Levant – but was already being cultivated in the Nile Valley by around 5000 BC, as scraps of fabric have been recovered from tombs of that date. Other fragments of cloth found in tombs of the Predynastic period (5500–3100 BC) testify that woollen yarn – from both sheep and goats – was also used, but wool was never as popular as linen. Cotton from India and imported silk did not reach Egypt until the Ptolemaic Dynasty (305–30 BC), while mohair, from the wool of the angora goat, was not introduced until the seventh century AD.

Getting the thread

The production of linen yarn from flax was a long, complicated process, beginning with the early harvesting of the flax; the younger the plant, the finer the fibres. Plants were pulled from the soil, rather than cut with a scythe, to maximize the length of the fibres. The dry stalks were soaked for several days to loosen their hard outer layers, then dried in the sun before being beaten to shreds and pulled through two sticks to clean the fibres of any woody detritus. The fibres were then hand-spun into yarn, a job usually reserved for women.

The weaver sits at the loom using a shuttle to weave the weft threads through those of the warp.

Lengths of yarn are being measured out to make warp threads for the loom.

The spinners gather their threads around the spindle below the whorl – a disc that acts as a flywheel.

▲ Linen from the New Kingdom
Depending on the thickness of the yarn, and the closeness of the weave, Egyptian linen could vary in quality from rather coarse, everyday stuff like this, to the sheer, diaphanous material used to make the clinging robes depicted in sculptures and reliefs.

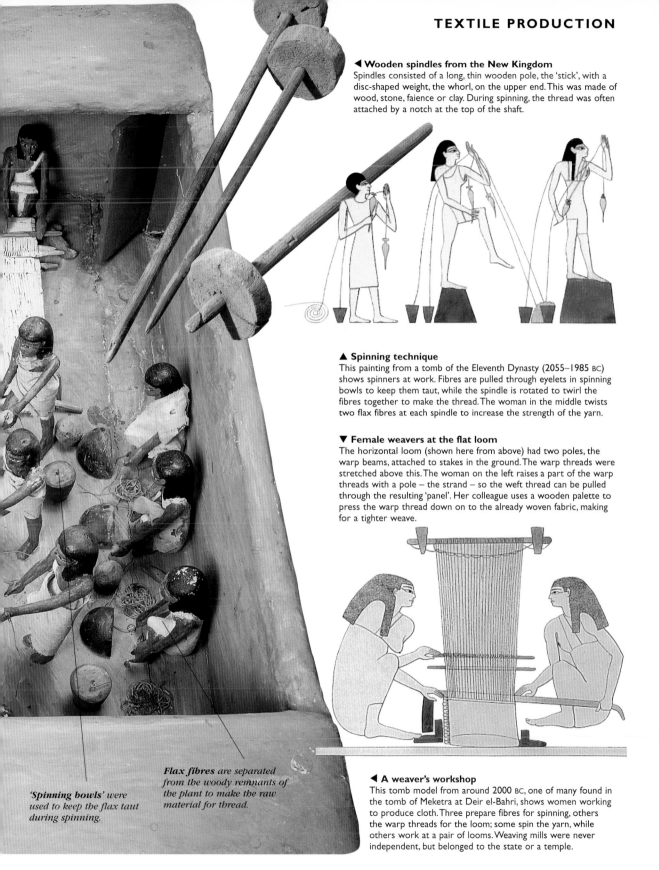

◀ Wooden spindles from the New Kingdom
Spindles consisted of a long, thin wooden pole, the 'stick', with a disc-shaped weight, the whorl, on the upper end. This was made of wood, stone, faience or clay. During spinning, the thread was often attached by a notch at the top of the shaft.

▲ Spinning technique
This painting from a tomb of the Eleventh Dynasty (2055–1985 BC) shows spinners at work. Fibres are pulled through eyelets in spinning bowls to keep them taut, while the spindle is rotated to twirl the fibres together to make the thread. The woman in the middle twists two flax fibres at each spindle to increase the strength of the yarn.

▼ Female weavers at the flat loom
The horizontal loom (shown here from above) had two poles, the warp beams, attached to stakes in the ground. The warp threads were stretched above this. The woman on the left raises a part of the warp threads with a pole – the strand – so the weft thread can be pulled through the resulting 'panel'. Her colleague uses a wooden palette to press the warp thread down on to the already woven fabric, making for a tighter weave.

Flax fibres are separated from the woody remnants of the plant to make the raw material for thread.

'Spinning bowls' were used to keep the flax taut during spinning.

◀ A weaver's workshop
This tomb model from around 2000 BC, one of many found in the tomb of Meketra at Deir el-Bahri, shows women working to produce cloth. Three prepare fibres for spinning, others the warp threads for the loom; some spin the yarn, while others work at a pair of looms. Weaving mills were never independent, but belonged to the state or a temple.

INSIGHT

A splash of colour

Coloured textiles were a rarity in Ancient Egypt before the New Kingdom (1550–1069 bc), when various dyeing techniques began to be used on a much larger scale. For pigment, the Egyptians used natural ochres to produce red, yellow and brown, and plant dyes such as woad for blue and sea-wort for red. Threads, rather than whole pieces of cloth, were dyed, and the colourful yarns were used to weave geometric patterns into fabrics (below left, on a piece of linen from Deir el-Medina), or to decorate the neckline or seam of a tunic. If the fabric was intended to robe someone of high rank from the royal household, figurative motifs might also be woven into it. In the Coptic period (between the division of the Roman Empire in AD 395 and the Islamic conquest of Egypt in AD 641), coloured cloth became abundant, as wool – much easier to dye than linen – was increasingly used for everyday purposes in Egypt. Robes of the time were decorated with wide ribbons and bands – with coloured, mainly figurative motifs woven into them (below, from the sixth or seventh century AD). As well as images from the natural world, motifs on textiles took inspiration from Christian symbolism or were based on Hellenistic geometric elements.

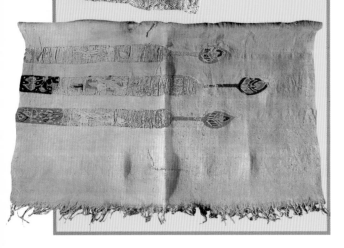

Two kinds of loom were used in Ancient Egypt. The horizontal flat loom, typically used by women, was the simpler of the two. Only the two poles of the warp beams had to be attached to the ground. The main drawback was that fabric woven on it could never be longer than the loom itself. The vertical upright loom – only used by men, according to tomb paintings – was more complicated. The two warp beams could be turned, allowing the weaver to roll up the woven fabric, and therefore make much longer bolts of cloth.

Weaving techniques

The prevalent technique used to make cloth was simple linen weaving, interlacing warp and weft threads. This one technique could produce a wide variety of cloth, depending on the thickness of the yarn and the quality of the weave. It was quite common to vary the pattern by bunching together two or three threads in the warp and weft, a style now known as panama weave. In the Eighteenth Dynasty (1550–1295 bc), a style now called gobelin weaving was introduced, where several coloured weft threads are used in producing figurative patterns.

The woven fabric was then washed and folded, and the quality of the finished cloth was categorized according to its sheerness and the looseness or density of the weave. The best quality went to make fine clothes; another grade was preferred for bandaging mummies, and so on for various other purposes.

◀ Mats and baskets
This relief shows plant stalks being prepared for weaving into a mat or basket. Egyptian basket- and rug-makers used a range of plants, mostly palm ribs and different types of reed, but also wheatstraw, halfa grass, raffia, bullrush and papyrus. Techniques of coiling, twining, weaving and plaiting were used. Reliefs and tomb paintings that show mats being made suggest that they were mainly the work of shepherds, who plaited them in the open air while watching over their flocks.

▶ A modern craft
Young Egyptians today learn techniques of making carpets and wall hangings very similar to those developed by their distant ancestors, knotting them or weaving them in what has become known as the gobelin technique. A rectangular, horizontal frame is used in this tapestry work. The warp threads are stretched across it, and the desired pattern is then either knotted in, using short lengths of coloured yarn, or woven into place using several small weaver's shuttles.

Baskets of material, newly wrung out, are taken away to be dried in the sun.

Washed cloth was wrung out by hand – usually by a man – to speed up the drying process.

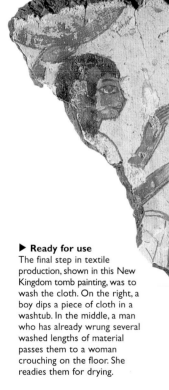

▶ Ready for use
The final step in textile production, shown in this New Kingdom tomb painting, was to wash the cloth. On the right, a boy dips a piece of cloth in a washtub. In the middle, a man who has already wrung several washed lengths of material passes them to a woman crouching on the floor. She readies them for drying.

Boiling water was used to wash the cloth, which was then sun-dried, a treatment that bleached it white.

Writing Materials

In Ancient Egypt, scribes recorded harvests, taxes and salaries, and transcribed sacred and secular texts. They were identified with the tools of their trade, which went with them to their tombs and were shown in reliefs and paintings.

Scribes carried the tools of their trade wherever they went – in the countryside, the granaries and even on the field of battle, where it was their duty, once the fighting was over, to count the number of enemy dead. The scribe's brushes, palette, pigments, papyri and other writing materials were stored in a box of wicker or wood – sometimes used as a writing support – or in a leather container for ease of transport.

The scribe's palette was a rectangular piece of wood (sometimes stone) some 30 x 6cm (12 x 2⅜in), with a central groove or slot to hold reed pens or brushes, and a couple of circular wells in one end. One was to hold red pigment, obtained from red ochre, and was used for headings and highlighting important words. The other was for a black pigment, based on charcoal or lamp black, in which the main text was written.

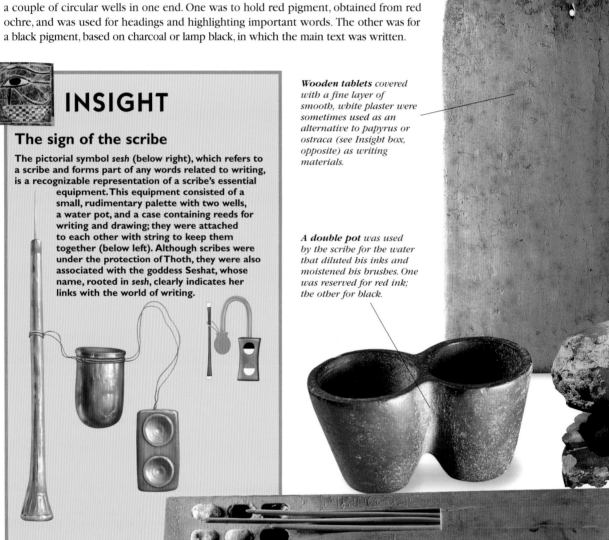

INSIGHT

The sign of the scribe

The pictorial symbol *sesh* (below right), which refers to a scribe and forms part of any words related to writing, is a recognizable representation of a scribe's essential equipment. This equipment consisted of a small, rudimentary palette with two wells, a water pot, and a case containing reeds for writing and drawing; they were attached to each other with string to keep them together (below left). Although scribes were under the protection of Thoth, they were also associated with the goddess Seshat, whose name, rooted in *sesh*, clearly indicates her links with the world of writing.

Wooden tablets covered with a fine layer of smooth, white plaster were sometimes used as an alternative to papyrus or ostraca (see Insight box, opposite) as writing materials.

A double pot was used by the scribe for the water that diluted his inks and moistened his brushes. One was reserved for red ink; the other for black.

The painters who created vignettes to decorate papyri, such as those in the *Book of the Dead*, required a wider range of colours, and had palettes with extra wells for blue, yellow, white or green pigment. Before beginning work, a scribe had to prepare his inks. Pigments were supplied in the form of bars or round 'cakes', from which a piece was broken off and reduced to powder using a stone crusher and mortar. The scribe then put a little pigment on to a wetted brush and mixed it with water on the palette to obtain the required consistency.

INSIGHT

Signed and sealed

The Egyptians who knew how to read and write – basically, the scribes or civil servants and various royal dignitaries (all of them men) – exchanged a great deal of correspondence. Clay tablets or ostraca (pieces of polished pottery or limestone) were often used for brief notes and functional letters, but more important communications were written on sheets of papyrus rolled or folded to form a letter, complete with the names of the sender and the addressee.

The letters were secured with personal seals pressed into a small piece of fresh clay. These seals were also attached to legal deeds, as a means of proving their authenticity. Hieroglyphs identifying the owner of a personal seal were cut into the seal's surface in order to leave a pattern in relief in the clay.

The seals took various forms. They were often found on the back of a scarab or set into a ring like a precious stone. Others were in a custom-made triangular form, with a hole for the finger (below). The cylinder seal, which was widespread in Mesopotamia at the time, was found less frequently in Egypt.

Royal seals were often made of precious metals, gold or silver, but the most usual and functional material was glazed earthenware, as in the seal below.

◀ **Scribe statues**
From the time of the Old Kingdom (2686–2181 BC), princes and other dignitaries commissioned statues that showed them sitting cross-legged in a posture associated with scribes, with a papyrus unrolled across their knees. Some are shown reading, as here, and some writing. The purpose of such statues was to imply that their subjects were scholars.

Natural pigments came in cakes that were first powdered, then mixed with water.

Small pigment pots stored the crushed materials ready for dilution and use.

This palette has six pigment wells and a slot to take the scribe's reed pens.

A flat mortar and a crusher were used to pulverize the pigments.

The writing material used by a scribe depended on the job he was doing. For notes that were not to be kept or for rough drafts, scribes used an ostracon, a piece of limestone or a fragment of pottery polished up for the purpose, or incised a text in wet clay. Children and apprentice scribes normally practised on wooden tablets covered with a layer of plaster.

Using papyrus

Generally, papyrus was reserved for administrative texts, religious books, letters and literary or scholarly works. It was costly to make and a far more valuable material than paper is today; unneeded texts were often erased so that the sheets could be re-used. Scribes used special tools to prepare papyrus. A wooden smoothing tool or polishing stone was rubbed over the sheets to ensure an even writing surface, while a bronze blade was used to cut pieces off the precious papyrus if it was to be used for a letter or inscription of only a few lines.

▼ **Domestic details**
The scribes of Deir-el-Medina, the village of the workers who built the tombs in the Valley of the Kings, left thousands of ostraca on which they noted trivial details of everyday life. These included reasons for the absence of workers, ration accounts and questions to the oracles. Today these texts are an invaluable insight into the lives and concerns of ordinary Egyptians.

Scribes at work

In Ancient Egypt, scribes found employment in just about every sector of the economy, including agriculture, crafts, trade, mining, building and quarrying. They were also an important part of life in the temples, where they were involved with copying and creating religious texts, and in the army, where they listed the conscripts, for instance. The model below comes from the tomb of Meketra, who lived under the pharaoh Mentuhotep III (2004–1992 BC), and shows scribes noting down the number of cattle raised by various farmers.

Papyrus rolls were used for the important business of the cattle census.

A supervisor oversees the scribes' work from a nearby seat under the colonnade.

The cross-legged position was not used by all scribes. This man has one knee raised and one leg folded beneath him.

The scribes' palettes, containing wells for red and black ink, have been carefully placed on the boxes in front of them.

▼ Storing papyri

Records written on papyri were protected from decay by keeping them in boxes or sealed vases. This jar successfully preserved documents in demotic Egyptian and Greek from the second century BC until today.

▶ Rough sketches

Writing materials were not just for documents. An artist has used this papyrus to sketch birds and animals. The grid of red ink over the drawings suggests they were intended to be copied onto another medium, such as a wall.

Making Papyrus

Paper is an Egyptian invention. While most modern paper is made from tree pulp, Egypt's writing materials were made from a reedy plant that grew abundantly in the swampy areas of the Nile Valley. The finished product was exported to the Middle East and Greece.

Great thickets of papyrus grew in the swamps and marshes of the Nile Valley, particularly in those of the Delta, from prehistory to throughout the time of the pharaohs. It was the heraldic plant of Lower Egypt, and is often depicted with the lotus, the heraldic plant of Upper Egypt, as a symbol of the unification of the country. The densely packed, reedy expanses provided a habitat for many species of birds and animals. Several tomb murals and reliefs show the teeming life among the papyrus as part of hunting and fishing scenes.

A versatile plant

The ancient Egyptians saw this reed – which grew so abundantly out of the life-giving mud of the Nile – as a symbol of youth and joy, but also found many practical uses for it. The lower part of the plant could be eaten as a vegetable, while the fibrous inner bark, or bast, was used to make rope, baskets and sandals, or was woven into a coarse cloth used for sails and the loincloths of the poor.

A genet – a small, cat-like carnivore – is hunting birds in the papyrus thickets.

This owl is protecting its young from an attack by potential predators.

▶ The scribes

From the time of the first pharaohs, rolls of papyrus were used by professional writers called scribes. They used reed brushes and red and black inks to write their texts in hieratic script, derived from hieroglyphics. In a land where few people were literate, scribes were the officials and administrators, members of the élite, and the profession was often passed from father to son.

Seated on the floor with his legs tucked beneath him, the scribe held the papyrus roll on his knees and rolled it to the right. His loincloth served as a pad as he wrote from right to left in single columns.

◄ The papyrus plant
The papyrus (*Cyperus papyrus*), which is a member of the reed-grass family, has stems that are triangular in section and grow up to 3m (10ft) tall. It was once common in the wetlands of the Nile, but the draining of the swamps and overcultivation in the past mean that, today, extensive areas of papyrus are found growing wild only in its upper reaches in Ethiopia and Sudan. Small areas are also cultivated in Egypt to make replica documents for tourists.

▼ The banks of the Nile
The tangled undergrowth of the muddy banks and swamps surrounding the Nile teemed with wildlife. It provided food and shelter for migratory birds, as well as native species, and the abundant birdlife in turn attracted other animals. Egyptian tomb paintings often return to the themes of hunting and fishing in the papyrus thickets. Pictures such as this appear in even the earliest tombs of the Ancient Kingdom, known as mastabas.

Brightly coloured butterflies represent the teeming insect life thriving in the papyrus.

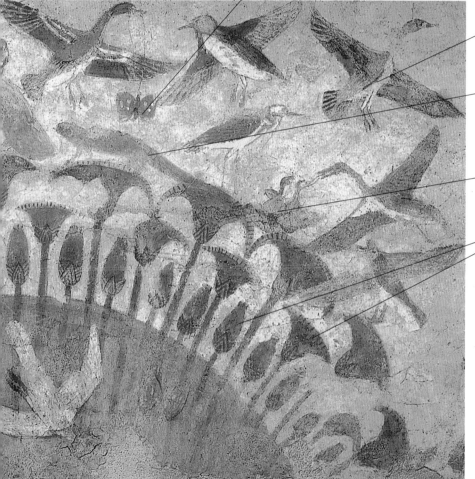

*A **wild duck** takes flight from the papyrus reeds.*

*An **ichneumon**, an African relative of the mongoose, creeps through the reed bed seeking its prey – small birds and eggs, as well as snakes.*

Several birds make their nests in the reed beds between the papyrus heads.

The leafy heads of the papyri are shown at various stages in their growth cycle.

▼ Stylized decoration
Stylized versions of the papyrus were often used as decorative motifs. The umbrella-shaped head of the plant (insignificant flowers rise from the centre of each rosette of leaves) changes shape as it grows. Open papyri and closed buds alike are shown in reliefs, paintings, amulets and jewellery, as well as in the capitals of stone columns, clustered together in long rows in imitation of the Nile's reed beds.

DOCUMENT

Making a papyrus roll

Making a roll of papyrus was a complex business involving a good deal of skilled labour. Papyrus was used primarily for important documents because of the costs of production. Scribes also wrote on leather sheets, on wood covered with plaster and – most inexpensive of all – on chips of limestone or broken pottery.

1. First, the stem was cut into pieces of roughly the same length, and the outer layers were peeled away. The inner pith was then cut lengthways into strips.

2. Two layers of strips went into each sheet of papyrus. Several strips were laid alongside each other, then another layer was laid at right angles to this. The two layers were not interwoven.

3. Both layers were moistened, then firmly beaten together, breaking down the fibres and gluing the layers together in a single sheet with a felt texture. This was left for several days, under weights, to dry out.

4. The final step was to use a flat stone to polish the sheets to a smooth writing surface, then to trim their edges. The finished sheets were glued together to make a roll ready for use.

The papyrus harvest

Fully grown papyrus plants were sought out by the harvesters.

Bundles of the stalks could be tied together to make lightweight boats or rafts. These were useful for hunting in the shallow waters, but did not last long, as the stems became waterlogged.

A pliable material

This ability to take up water was a positive advantage in the most important use of the plant. The pith of the stems was fashioned into a fine, pale and pliable writing material that was used in Egypt from at least the time of the First Dynasty – the oldest surviving piece of papyrus is from a tomb of about 3000 BC – until the final takeover of paper some 4,000 years later.

The name of the plant is a testament to its importance. 'Papyrus' derives from *pa-en-per-aa*, 'belonging to the pharaoh'. The king had a monopoly over the manufacture and sale of papyrus for writing materials. Although the plant was grown from seed in Cyprus, Palestine and Sicily in ancient times, Egypt – its natural home – remained the principal source of fine writing materials for the whole of the Mediterranean region.

Freshly cut papyrus stems are bundled together to be taken back to the river bank.

▲ A valuable resource
Papyrus was the most important writing material for officials recording economic transactions, and for literary texts. Completed rolls were stored in large jars to protect them from insects and the weather. While officials generally wrote only on one side, papyrus rolls were so expensive that they were often recycled (sometimes much later) by writing on the back.

Boats made from papyrus stems lashed with papyrus rope carried the harvesters through the marshes.

Muddy, waterlogged soil provides the ideal growing medium for the reed-like papyrus plant.

Surprisingly little is known for certain about the cultivation of papyrus, but it is reasonable to assume it was harvested, as it is now, mainly in spring or summer. Murals and reliefs from Ancient Egypt show how the stalks were pulled from the water, cut and transported in bundles to the workshops (see above).

Complicated process

Fresh papyri, in good condition, were needed to create fine quality writing material. Strips of the inner part of the stems were compressed into sheets that were usually no more than 45cm (18in) long. These sheets were then fixed together to form rolls of varying lengths. The standard roll of papyrus had around 20 sheets, but they could be more extensive; the longest known roll is over 40m (130ft) long. The inside of a papyrus roll was written on first; the other side was often left blank.

INSIGHT

Papyrus today

In the first millennium AD, papyrus was slowly replaced as a writing material first by parchment, then by paper. Today, however, tourists can buy papyri made and inscribed with ancient motifs (below), using similar methods to those in Ancient Egypt.

Ceramics

Although individual pots tend to be fragile, broken pieces of ceramic survive for millennia, providing a vital archaeological resource.

Clay vessels are of special interest to archaeologists, providing them with basic information about the ancient sites that they are excavating. A particular shape of vessel, for example, can identify a building as a grain store or a temple. Evolving design styles and manufacturing methods mean that pieces of broken pot - potsherds - can accurately date the graves or dwellings where they are found. Local and national variations in clay and design mean that they can also give us insights into patterns of national and international trade.

▶ Firing and colour
Pots made of Nile clay are naturally reddish-brown when they are fired in the presence of air, as in a kiln. Robbing the clay of oxygen as it bakes gives the pot a black finish.

▶ Handmade
Ceramics were hand-raised before the potter's wheel was introduced in the Fifth Dynasty (2494–2345 BC). Funerary models continued to be handmade, and the ancient technique of building up large vessels using coils of rolled clay was still used.

▼ Storage vessels
Stone vessels were used for temple or funerary offerings, but earthenware was employed almost exclusively for everyday purposes. These army recruits are receiving their allocation of provisions in the form of jars of beer and basket-shaped vessels piled high with food.

Ceramic shapes were more varied in the New Kingdom, influenced by vessels brought from overseas. This tall jar is typical of the Eighteenth Dynasty (1550-1295 BC).

◀ The materials
These pots represent two types of clay used in ceramics by the Ancient Egyptians. The one on the far left is made from the alluvial clay found all along the Nile Valley. This is a dark, blackish-brown clay that dries to a grey-brown. Firing gives it its distinctive reddish-brown hue. Although this clay produced pots with a rather coarse finish, it was by far the most popular material, with almost all everyday items being made of it. The other pot is fashioned from limestone-rich marl (clay with stone in it) that was found in just a few places in Upper Egypt, particularly around Qena. The raw marl is light grey in colour, but changes to yellow-green or pink on firing, depending on the temperature. The silica content in the clay gave the wares a polished finish.

▼ Faience and glazed soapstone
Before they began to make complete objects in faience, such as this glazed hippo, the Egyptians carved models in steatite, or soapstone, then covered them with a paste of powdered quartz, limestone and copper oxide. When heated, it formed a thin green or blue decorative coating.

Amphora supports, which were necessary if the round-bottomed pots were to stand upright, sometimes took the form of a ring set into a wooden trestle base.

Ceramic vessels were used mainly for serving, storing and transporting drinks and foodstuffs.

Egyptian potters produced mainly vessels – small tableware such as cups and goblets, as well as larger storage jars and amphoras. The hand-turned potter's wheel arrived in the Fifth Dynasty (2494–2345 BC), but came into its own only when the assisted wheel was introduced in the Second Intermediate period (1650–1550 BC). An assistant powering and stabilizing the wheel meant that the potter could use both hands, and faster rotation brought centrifugal force into play in shaping the pots. As a result, pots in the New Kingdom (1550–1069 BC) became slimmer and more elegant, with better formed rims. This time was also the high point of pot decoration. Although the Ancient Egyptians did not use glazes in the modern sense, by the end of the Eighteenth Dynasty they were decorating their pots with geometric or figurative designs applied in paint or slip or incised into the clay.

Making pots

Tomb decorations show how Egyptian potters worked. Cleaned clay was watered and kneaded with the feet to the right consistency. Chopped straw made it more solid and less sticky. Modelled pieces were set aside to dry. When they were 'leather-hard', the potter would decorate them, perhaps smoothing the surface with a pebble, or cutting in a pattern and filling it with a slip of clay in a contrasting colour. Pots were finished by firing – at first in an open fire, but later in kilns at a temperature of 500°–600°C (932°–1112°F).

▼ Canopic jars
Potters and makers of stone vessels had certain common items in their repertoires. Canopic jars, made for the storage of the viscera of the dead, were usually stone – such as these in painted limestone – but were sometimes also made in earthenware. The lids, shaped to represent either the head of the deceased or one of the Four Sons of Horus, were always made of the same material as the jars.

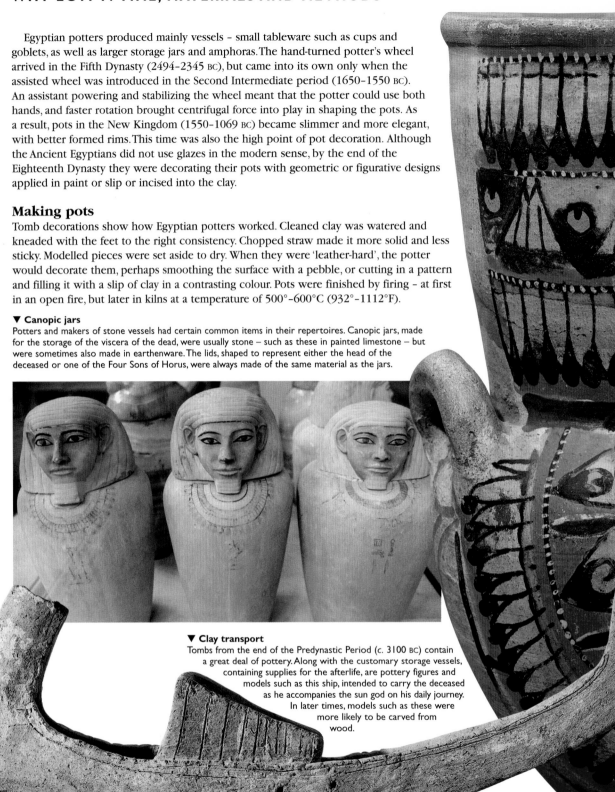

▼ Clay transport
Tombs from the end of the Predynastic Period (c. 3100 BC) contain a great deal of pottery. Along with the customary storage vessels, containing supplies for the afterlife, are pottery figures and models such as this ship, intended to carry the deceased as he accompanies the sun god on his daily journey. In later times, models such as these were more likely to be carved from wood.

◀ Bold colours
In the New Kingdom (1550–1069 BC), potters decorated their wares with geometric patterns, or exuberant depictions of plants and flowers, all painted in vivid colours. Vessels recovered from tombs, such as this two-handled jar, or amphora, find their exact match in the scenes of feasting and offerings that were common in tomb paintings of the time.

▼ Modelled decoration
The New Kingdom saw a great flowering of decorated pottery. By the end of the period, multicoloured floral or figurative decorations adorned the upper areas of most vessels, while large amphorae often had models such as this antelope's head attached for purely decorative reasons.

▲ Double containers
This ingenious and well-proportioned double vase is a product of the inventive potters of the New Kingdom, but makes use of a design from the Predynastic period and subsequently found in every period of Ancient Egyptian history.

◀ Rounded bases
Many Egyptian containers had a rounded or pointed base – easier for potters to achieve than a flat one – and were designed to be hung from a beam in a house and transported in nets. Sometimes they were placed in a support made of palm leaves, clay or wood.

INSIGHT

Predynastic pots

In the early nineteenth century, the English archaeologist Flinders Petrie developed a typology for pre- and early historical Egyptian pottery, categorizing finds by date and location. With few exceptions, Petrie's classification is still in use today.

Ceramics from Egypt's Predynastic period (5500–3100 BC) impress most of all through their high quality and richness of design. They are grouped into different styles, according to their culture of origin. The oldest cultures of Upper Egypt were named after finds of ceramics at Tasa and Badari, dating from 5500–4000 BC. Of particular interest are the tulip-shaped containers found at the cemetery at Tasa, with engraved geometric designs. These are similar to finds from Nubia. The mainly thin-walled pots of the Badarian culture

▼ This dark red, tulip-shaped container is decorated with a geometric pattern cut in the clay before firing. It is typical of the Tasa culture, named for the site of an important archaeological find of ceramics. Similar pots were also found further south, in Nubia.

▼ ▼ The red-brown colour, with black lip and inner surface, of this cup is typical of the Badarian culture. They made their pots from very light, sanded clay and fired them at very high temperatures. The black colour was achieved by taking the hot pot directly from the fire and plunging it into ashes.

have a highly polished surface; most vessels are dark red with a black upper band, indicating they were placed upside down in ashes after they were fired. Their smooth, shiny surface was probably obtained by polishing the moulded pot with fine pebbles, or strips of leather, before the clay was completely dry.

The later Naqada culture was also named after an archeological site where a significant find of ceramics was made. This culture can be divided into two phases. Pots of the Naqada I period (4000–3500 BC) have a dark red, polished surface with white decorations, in which, for the first time, people and animals occasionally appear. Naqada II pottery (3500–3100 BC) typically has light pink or yellow pots with figurative or geometric decorations in dark brown. Dark red pots with a black upper band also appear in this period.

◄ The dark red, polished surface, decorated with patterns in a pale slip, is typical of the Naqada I, or Amratian, period (4000–3500 BC).

▼ This full-bodied container, made from a pale-coloured clay decorated in dark red, is from the Naqada II, or Gerzean, period (3500–3100 BC). It has handles and is painted with guinea fowl around a large, flowering plant.

◄ Egyptian faience

Egyptian faience is named for its resemblance to mediaeval Italian, blue-and-white, tin-glazed earthenware. The name is misleading, however, as Egyptian faience is not a true ceramic. It was produced by firing a mixture of pulverized quartz, or quartz sand, with a little lime and natron (a natural carbonate of sodium), water and sometimes gum arabic. The addition of metal salts gave it a colourful, glassy finish, and the Ancient Egyptians called it *tjehenet*, literally bright or dazzling. Its main use was in making jewels, as well as ornaments and small vessels.

▲ Creating colour 'glazes'

Egyptian faience took its colour from the copper oxide added to the basic mix before the piece was modelled. In the heat of the kiln, the copper oxide and alkali salts from the natron migrate to the surface to form the blue-green coating. Other 'glazes' were created in the New Kingdom by substituting different metals for copper. Lead and antimony gave yellow, and cobalt a rich, deep blue.

INSIGHT

Nubian ceramics

In Nubia, north of modern-day Khartoum, pottery of a very high quality was being produced by the late sixth millennium BC. These early pots were decorated with engraved patterns of undulating lines and geometric shapes marked out in dots.

The similarity of Nubian forms to Egyptian ones suggests a good deal of contact with the so-called 'A group' of Nubian culture (3700–2800 BC). Red and brown pots with black upper rims, similar to those of the Egyptian Badarian period, were popular. Egyptian pots of this time possessed rounded bottoms or small, flat standing areas, but the

Nubian pots mostly had a pointed base. The Nubian C group culture (2300–1550 BC), produced vessels with flatter bases (above); the design is created by using a contrasting colour to fill in a pattern cut into a polished finish.

The finest Ancient Nubian pottery came from the kingdom of Kerma (c. 2500–1500 BC). Its tulip-shaped vases, their black rims separated from the red lower body by a brilliant grey band, reveal the potters' mastery in their very thin walls and polished finish.

Pots from later periods showed increasing influence from Egypt, Greece and Rome. Vessels of the Meroitic period (300 BC–AD 350), for example, often have painted decoration in a decidedly Mediterranean style, as in the freely expressed floral border on the bowl below.

The Written Word

Well before the unification of ancient Egypt, smaller kingdoms developed written and pictorial communication systems. After unification, an army of well-organized scribes, as well as sculptors and engravers, recorded the details of life, from trade and travel to religion and warfare.

To us, the scribes' hieroglyphs and hieratic script are both visual treasures and historical gems. But as kingdoms expanded making administration and organisation more complex, they were also a necessity. Recording and listing became vital functions, and through these records we have access to a treasure of information.

But writing had even greater significance than this to Ancient Egyptians. It was important in death. Until the end of the Middle Kingdom in about 1650 B.C.E., only the king had the right to move smoothly into the Afterlife. Everyone else had to adorn their coffins with instructions for spells, lists of offerings to the gods, and appeasements of all kinds. At the end of the Middle Kingdom, the written route to the Afterlife was encapsulated in one reference: the Book of the Dead.

Literacy was not merely a functional cataloguing and labelling tool. It could also be descriptive and lyrical. The pyramid of Pepy I (2321–2287 B.C.E.) was described variously as 'established and beautiful' and 'perfect and eternal' – epithets that have a great poetic serenity to them. Writing had meaning, beauty and clarity – a lasting treasure.

The Weighing of the Heart
Detail from the wooden coffin of Nespawershepi, chief scribe of the Temple of Amun, showing the weighing of the heart in the Hall of Judgement. The owner (right) watches as his heart is weighed against the feather of Truth (Maat). Anubis adjusts the scales while Thoth records the result.

Hieratic Script

Several different scripts developed from Egyptian hieroglyphs. One of the most important, called 'hieratic' by the Greeks, was the everyday writing in Egypt for nearly 2,000 years.

Hieroglyphs, the most famous and earliest type of Egyptian writing, were well suited to monumental inscriptions, but not to everyday use. Hieratic writing, which developed from them, is a script. Its more rounded outline made for quicker, more flowing writing.

Simplified signs

The hieratic signs that appeared around the end of the Early Dynastic period (*c.* 2686 BC) were simplifications of hieroglyphs. Although the original hieroglyphs can still be identified, the hieratic shapes are less precise and complex, and can be joined together, unlike hieroglyphs, which always have a space between them. The difference between hieratic script and hieroglyphs is similar to that between handwriting and printed capital letters. Hieratic remained the Egyptians' everyday script until it was replaced by demotic in the seventh century BC.

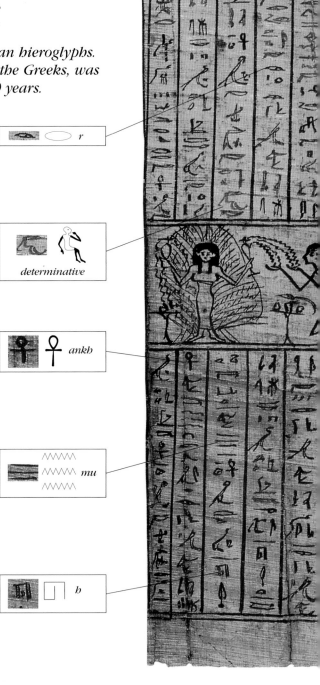

r

determinative

ankh

mu

h

◀ **Remarkable longevity**
Hieroglyphs were used throughout pharaonic history. For much of this time, the number of symbols used was relatively small, but in the Ptolemaic and Roman periods it grew from 700 or so to around 6,000. This form of writing became extinct only with the closure of the Egyptian temples by the Romans in the fourth century AD.

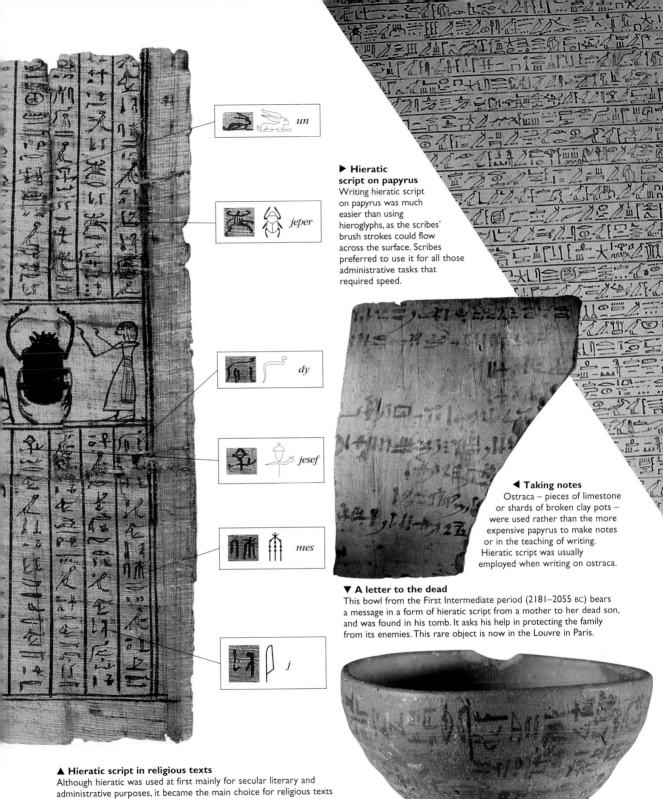

un

jeper

dy

jesef

mes

j

▶ Hieratic script on papyrus
Writing hieratic script on papyrus was much easier than using hieroglyphs, as the scribes' brush strokes could flow across the surface. Scribes preferred to use it for all those administrative tasks that required speed.

◀ Taking notes
Ostraca – pieces of limestone or shards of broken clay pots – were used rather than the more expensive papyrus to make notes or in the teaching of writing. Hieratic script was usually employed when writing on ostraca.

▼ A letter to the dead
This bowl from the First Intermediate period (2181–2055 BC) bears a message in a form of hieratic script from a mother to her dead son, and was found in his tomb. It asks his help in protecting the family from its enemies. This rare object is now in the Louvre in Paris.

▲ Hieratic script in religious texts
Although hieratic was used at first mainly for secular literary and administrative purposes, it became the main choice for religious texts after Alexander the Great conquered Egypt in 332 BC and ushered in 300 years of Greek rule. This example is from the *Book of the Dead*.

From the beginning, hieratic was a completely phonetic script, with each sign representing a sound rather than a word or idea. It was always written from right to left. Before the Eleventh Dynasty (2055-1985 BC), the symbols were usually arranged in columns; after that date, they were written in horizontal lines.

Scribes often developed individual styles of writing, but in the Middle Kingdom (2055-1650 BC), two noticeably different types of hieratic script evolved. In literary texts, the signs were precisely written and more attractive to look at, while 'abnormal hieratic', used in administrative and economic documents and texts, employed more flowing and schematic signs for speed of writing. During the New Kingdom (1550-1069 BC), the signs were further rounded and simplified, becoming more and more 'polished'.

The beginning of demotic

An even simpler and more cursive script, called demotic by the Greeks and 'sekh shat' (writing for documents) by the Egyptians, developed out of abnormal hieratic. In the Twenty-Sixth Dynasty (664-525 BC), it replaced hieratic, except in sacred or funerary texts, which were still written in the 'literary' style. Hieratic was used for this purpose well into the Ptolemaic period (332-30 BC), and the Greeks, unaware of its mainly secular history, gave the script the name 'hieratic' (priestly), to distinguish it from demotic writing.

Hieroglyph	Hieratic	Transcription	Hieroglyph	Hieratic	Transcription	Hieroglyph	Hieratic	Transcription
		a			p			s
		j			f			sch
		jj / y			m			q
		a			n			k
		u, w			r			g
		b			ḫ			t
					ḥ			ṯ, t
					ẖ			d
					ḫ			ḏ

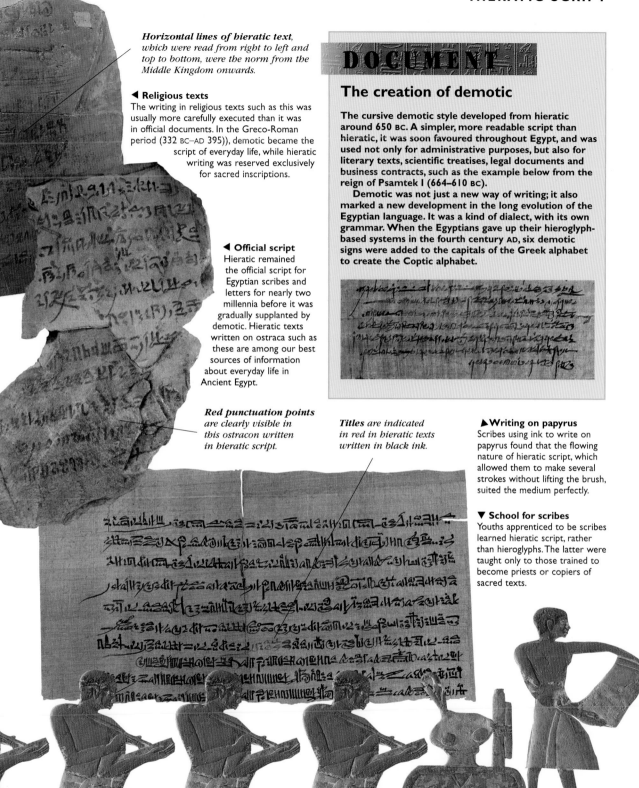

Horizontal lines of hieratic text, which were read from right to left and top to bottom, were the norm from the Middle Kingdom onwards.

◄ Religious texts
The writing in religious texts such as this was usually more carefully executed than it was in official documents. In the Greco-Roman period (332 BC–AD 395)), demotic became the script of everyday life, while hieratic writing was reserved exclusively for sacred inscriptions.

◄ Official script
Hieratic remained the official script for Egyptian scribes and letters for nearly two millennia before it was gradually supplanted by demotic. Hieratic texts written on ostraca such as these are among our best sources of information about everyday life in Ancient Egypt.

Red punctuation points are clearly visible in this ostracon written in hieratic script.

Titles are indicated in red in hieratic texts written in black ink.

DOCUMENT

The creation of demotic

The cursive demotic style developed from hieratic around 650 BC. A simpler, more readable script than hieratic, it was soon favoured throughout Egypt, and was used not only for administrative purposes, but also for literary texts, scientific treatises, legal documents and business contracts, such as the example below from the reign of Psamtek I (664–610 BC).

Demotic was not just a new way of writing; it also marked a new development in the long evolution of the Egyptian language. It was a kind of dialect, with its own grammar. When the Egyptians gave up their hieroglyph-based systems in the fourth century AD, six demotic signs were added to the capitals of the Greek alphabet to create the Coptic alphabet.

►Writing on papyrus
Scribes using ink to write on papyrus found that the flowing nature of hieratic script, which allowed them to make several strokes without lifting the brush, suited the medium perfectly.

▼ School for scribes
Youths apprenticed to be scribes learned hieratic script, rather than hieroglyphs. The latter were taught only to those trained to become priests or copiers of sacred texts.

The Egyptian Alphabet

Egyptian hieroglyphic writing is a pictorial script with a huge number of characters: 24 of these stand for what we would recognize as letters; others stand for complete words or combinations of consonants.

The earliest known use of hieroglyphs, the Ancient Egyptian form of writing, dates from around 3200 BC; the last inscription was in AD 394. For much of this time, the Egyptians relied on around 1,000 signs, although this increased sixfold in the Ptolemaic (332–30 BC) and Roman (30 BC–AD 395) periods.

The first step towards transforming Egyptian from a spoken to a written language was to use stylized word pictures - known as logograms - to represent objects or ideas. The word 'mouth', for example, was represented by a picture of two parted lips, while a wavy line was used to represent the word for water.

Pictures into sound

While this was fine for most common nouns and some verbs, there were real problems in representing such abstract concepts as 'luck', 'health' or 'life', or actions such as 'think' or 'do'. The solution was to adapt certain logograms to represent sounds, rather than things, so that

| *f* | *p* | *r* | *ḫ* | *t* |

these 'difficult' words could be spelled out phonetically. These 'sound signs', or phonograms, made up a sort of alphabet, although there are many more signs in Ancient Egyptian than in modern alphabets.

The Ancient Egyptian language was written entirely without any signs representing vowels. In this way, the language resembles Hebrew and Arabic, both of which are written as true consonant scripts. One sign suffices for all words with the same sequence of consonants, even words with quite different meanings, although we can assume they were actually pronounced differently.

| *rᶜ* | *s3* | *sw* | *mn* | *mr* |

Although we can never be sure exactly how Ancient Egyptian sounded, we can get an approximate idea by studying Coptic, the language that grew out of it. Coptic,

▶ **Expressions of immortality**
Hieroglyphic inscriptions on temple walls, graves and other monuments were both decorative and sacred, always destined 'for eternity'. Parts of the text of the *Book of the Dead*, for example, were inscribed on sarcophagi.

This illustration shows a fragment of the sarcophagus of Djed-Thoth-ef-Ankh, preserved in the Egyptian Museum in Turin, with a selection of the hieroglyphs explained. Here the text runs up and down in columns, while in other cases hieroglyphs were written on horizontal lines, usually, but not always, from right to left.

This phonetic sign represents the consonant m

This sign is a determinative, meaning to 'go forwards'

This sign represents the consonant n

This phonogram represents two consonants, written as ḏ3

The hieroglyph for 'man' is used here as a determinative

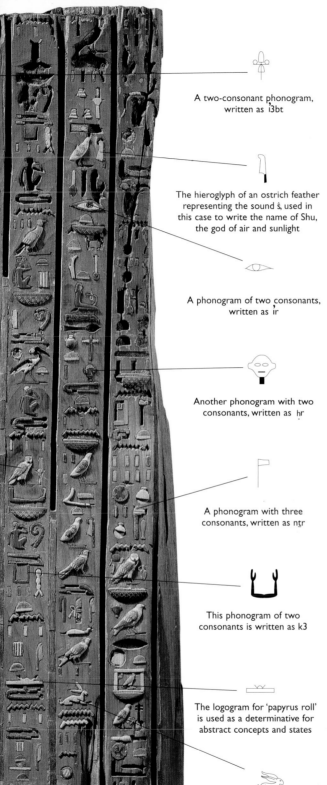

 A two-consonant phonogram, written as i3bt

 The hieroglyph of an ostrich feather representing the sound š, used in this case to write the name of Shu, the god of air and sunlight

 A phonogram of two consonants, written as ir

 Another phonogram with two consonants, written as hr

 A phonogram with three consonants, written as ntr

This phonogram of two consonants is written as k3

The logogram for 'papyrus roll' is used as a determinative for abstract concepts and states

This two-consonant phonogram of a hare is written wn

which is written in the Greek alphabet and some signs from demotic (the everyday script that was used from about 600 BC), and used vowels, is the closest connection we have to the long-dead language of Ancient Egypt.

New meanings

Phonograms were taken from the existing supply of logograms. The chosen ones lost their distinctive pictorial

 bit   *'nh*   *nfr*   *chc*   *hpr*

meaning, but gained a new value as a sound. There were 24 signs for single consonants in the hieroglyphic alphabet. Each came from a logogram for a word pronounced in the Ancient Egyptian language with that consonant. The sign for 'mouth', for example, stood for the sound 'r', and that for 'water' for the sound 'n'. The Ancient Egyptian alphabet also contained about 100 phonograms representing two consonant sounds, such as 'pr' or 'mn', and around 50 more representing a series of three consonants, such as 'nfr' or 'bit'. In order to vocalize these multi-consonant signs, Egyptologists put an 'e' between each one; 'nfr' is pronounced 'nefer'. Some of these consonants do not exist in English and cannot be directly transcribed into the our Roman alphabet. Additional points and strokes, known as diacritical signs, are used to express many of them.

Determinatives

A third category of sign found in hieroglyphic writing is the 'determinative'. These characters – which, like phonograms, were based on logograms – were put at

child   *eat/think*   *god*   *Uraeus/goddess*   *town*

the end of words written in phonograms to differentiate words that would otherwise look exactly the same. A word for a person, for example, would be followed by the sign for a man or a woman, while a verb of movement would be accompanied by a pair of running legs. As any group of consonants can represent several different words, making sense of an inscription depends both on context and the correct interpretation of determinatives.

Determinatives also help comprehension in another way. As they invariably appeared at the end of words (as hieroglyphs generally read from right to left, this means on the left), they served to separate words from one another. Otherwise, Ancient Egyptian completely lacks word spacing and indeed any sort of punctuation.

THE ALPHABET

SIGN	WRITTEN	SPOKEN	PICTURE MEANING
	3	*a*	*vulture*
	ỉ	*i* or *y*	*reed*
	c	*a*	*forearm*
	w	*w* or *u*	*quail chick*
	b	*b*	*foot*
	p	*p*	*stool*
	f	*f*	*horned viper*
	m	*m*	*owl*
	n	*n*	*water*
	r	*r*	*mouth*
	ḥ	*h*	*courtyard*
	ḥ	*h*	*rope*
	ḫ	*kh*	*placenta*
	ẖ	*kh*	*the belly and tail of an animal*
	s	*s*	*bolt (for a door)*
	ś	*s*	*folded cloth*
	š	*sh*	*pond*
	ḳ	*k*	*hill slope*
	k	*k*	*basket*
	g	*g*	*stand (for a vessel)*
	t	*t*	*loaf*
	ṯ	*tj*	*tethering rope*
	d	*d*	*hand*
	ḏ	*dj*	*cobra*

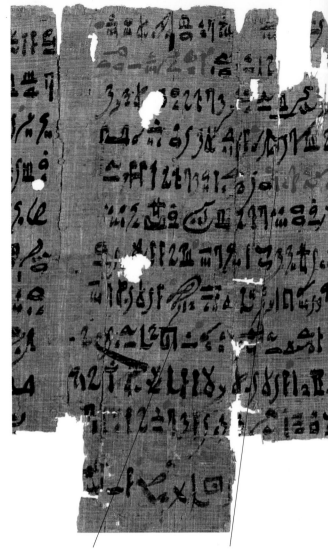

This single consonant sign has the value ḥ.

Characters in red indicate the start of a new section.

While hieroglyphs were mainly used for inscribing religious texts, especially tombs, the scribes adopted the hieratic script for more everyday purposes. This flowing script, based on the hieroglyphs, was used in business and administration from around 2700 BC.

Holy and eternal

It may seem remarkable that such a complex, unwieldy system should survive for so long. This may be because the long years of study required to master it contributed to the privileged, élite position of the scribes, or because hieroglyphs were seen as a gift from the gods; to alter or abandon them was seen as an act of sacrilege.

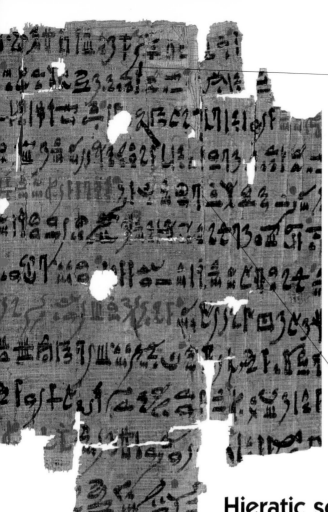

The horizontal layout of the hieroglyphs helps to date the papyrus.

◀ **Everyday writing**
The simplified form of writing, known as hieratic script, was developed for practical, everyday use. The majority of the papyrus texts that have come down to us are in hieratic script.

Until the Middle Kingdom (2055–1650 BC), it was written in columns. After this period, the script was generally laid out in horizontal lines from right to left, as here.

This character for š is more or less identical to the hieroglyph.

Hieratic script

This pictorial script was used to record business transactions and could be written more rapidly than the cumbersome hieroglyphs.

▲ **Writing and the gods**
The Egyptians believed that Thoth, the ibis-headed god of wisdom, and the goddess Seshat gave them the hieroglyphic system. Many of the phonetic characters have magical or symbolic meaning, in addition to their literal one, and were used for amulets, for example; this dual function is preserved in the word 'hieroglyph', which comes from the Greek, and means 'sacred carving'.

DOCUMENT

The cartouche

While Ancient Egyptian writing generally lacks punctuation, there is one convention that was of great use to early translators, such as François Chabas (1817–1882, right). This was the habit, from the Fourth Dynasty (2613–2494 BC) onwards, of enclosing the birth names and throne names of pharaohs in an oval shape that represented a loop of rope. When Napoleon mounted his expedition into Egypt in the early years of the nineteenth century, his soldiers dubbed the device a cartouche, or cartridge, because of its bullet shape.

With the phonograms for the royal names written in a cartouche – the one at near right is for Tutankhamun – the process of deciphering and reading hieroglyphs was greatly speeded up.

Reading Hieroglyphs

Hieroglyphs on monuments and papyri combine both art and language, and are arranged in different ways. The direction in which they are read follows certain rules, although there are exceptions.

Ancient Egyptian hieroglyphs are found in texts from the beginning of pharaonic times, around 3000 BC. They were written in rows, which could be read from left to right or right to left, or were arranged in columns, which were read from top to bottom. To work out the direction in which a particular text is to be read, it is necessary to look at the animal or human figures, which always face to the right or the left. If the figure faces right, the hieroglyphs are read from right to left, and vice versa.

Exceptions to the rule

These rules were sometimes broken, however, because of the artistic nature of hieroglyphs and their religious and symbolic significance. When replicating texts that most people recognized – such as sacred texts or offerings formulae – a harmonious composition was deemed more important than the strict rules of orientation.

▲ **Writing in columns**
On the walls of temples and tombs, hieroglyphic script generally appears in columns. The example above, from the Ptolemaic period (332–30 BC), is read from right to left.

The goose is shown facing right, meaning that this section of text is read from right to left.

The sun disc divides the inscription into two parts written in opposite directions.

The bee faces left, indicating that this part of the text is read from left to right.

◀ **Writing in lines**
Hieroglyphs were also written in horizontal lines, as on this pyramidion of Amenemhat III (1855–1808 BC) which is from his complex at Dahshur. This striking example illustrates the versatility of the hieroglyphic script, arranged here in two different directions.

DOCUMENT

Orientation of other ancient scripts

When Egypt was conquered by the Greeks and Romans, the Egyptians adopted their languages, both of which are written from left to right (below right, in a Latin manuscript). Coptic, the language of the Christian period (c. AD 395–641), combined the Greek alphabet with six further signs taken from demotic (a cursive Egyptian script) and was also written from left to right. After the Islamic conquest in the seventh century, Arabic became the national language, and remains so today. Arabic (below centre, in an extract from the Koran) is read from right to left. A number of other modern writing systems, such as Chinese and Japanese, are orientated this way. The text below left is Chinese, arranged in columns and read from right to left.

▲ **Changing direction**
There are instances where hieroglyphs are orientated in the opposite direction to the one that the figure is facing. This is sometimes found where standardized inscriptions are used, such as in offerings formulae. In the example above, the hieroglyphs are read from right to left.

▲ **Horizontal rows**
On this relief, the hieroglyphs are written in horizontal rows. As all the figures face right, each of the six rows is read from right to left.

Two horizontal lines of hieroglyphs decorate the base of Amenemhat's pyramidion.

Hieroglyphs from Life

To create the signs for their writing, the Ancient Egyptians took their inspiration from the world around them. They transformed animals, plants, natural elements, household objects and buildings into hieroglyphs.

A round 2000 BC, there were some 700 hieroglyphs in 25 categories, as well as a group of unidentified signs. When forming the signs that comprised their writing system, the Ancient Egyptians rejected the use of abstraction, and took the many elements that became hieroglyphs from the world around them.

Elements from everyday life

The most complete sections are those devoted to people and to parts of the human body, but animals and birds form another important category. Other groups include tools used by peasants and craftsmen, weapons for hunting or warfare, boats, crowns, jewels and sceptres.

The objects of everyday life, such as furniture, tables or food, form other groups, as do the sky and the sun. Buildings were represented in plan and elevation and, as new forms and functions were created, a hieroglyph

▲ **The forearm**
This denotes the phonetic sign 'ain', which is conventionally pronounced 'a'.

▲ **The owl**
This depicts the phonogram 'm'.

▲ **The horned viper**
This dangerous animal expresses the sound 'f'.

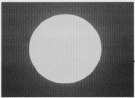

▲ **The sun**
The solar disc is shown as a circle with a dot in the centre. It is pronounced 'ra'.

DOCUMENT

The scarab

The symbol of rebirth, the scarab, in the form of a dung beetle, is the hieroglyph used to denote the word 'kheper', meaning 'becoming or transforming oneself'. The dung beetle (*Scarabeus sacer*) rolls a ball – the shape of which is a reminder of the solar star – from which it takes its nourishment and in which it lays its eggs. When associated with the solar disc, the word kheper designates the transformations of Ra. The sun disappears at night as an old man into the underworld and is reborn on the horizon in the morning as a scarab.

◀ **The beetle pushes a ball of dung with its hind legs.**

◀ **The throne name of Thutmose III, Menkheperra, means 'Longevity is the manifestation of Ra'.**

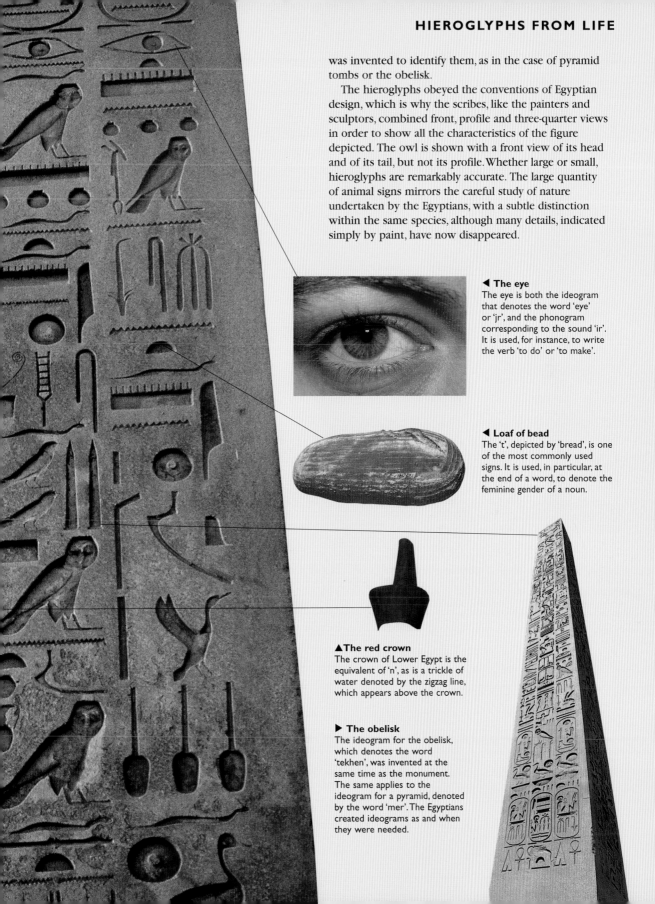

was invented to identify them, as in the case of pyramid tombs or the obelisk.

The hieroglyphs obeyed the conventions of Egyptian design, which is why the scribes, like the painters and sculptors, combined front, profile and three-quarter views in order to show all the characteristics of the figure depicted. The owl is shown with a front view of its head and of its tail, but not its profile. Whether large or small, hieroglyphs are remarkably accurate. The large quantity of animal signs mirrors the careful study of nature undertaken by the Egyptians, with a subtle distinction within the same species, although many details, indicated simply by paint, have now disappeared.

◄ **The eye**
The eye is both the ideogram that denotes the word 'eye' or 'jr', and the phonogram corresponding to the sound 'ir'. It is used, for instance, to write the verb 'to do' or 'to make'.

◄ **Loaf of bead**
The 't', depicted by 'bread', is one of the most commonly used signs. It is used, in particular, at the end of a word, to denote the feminine gender of a noun.

▲**The red crown**
The crown of Lower Egypt is the equivalent of 'n', as is a trickle of water denoted by the zigzag line, which appears above the crown.

► **The obelisk**
The ideogram for the obelisk, which denotes the word 'tekhen', was invented at the same time as the monument. The same applies to the ideogram for a pyramid, denoted by the word 'mer'. The Egyptians created ideograms as and when they were needed.

Temple Inscriptions

The hieroglyphic texts accompanying the reliefs on temple walls are much valued by Egyptologists as they describe what is going on. Their original purpose, though – like that of the images they accompany – was essentially magical, rather than informative.

Egyptian temples were not places of congregation and prayer like churches or mosques. Access to the temples was forbidden to ordinary Egyptians; hieroglyphs were not intended to edify casual visitors.

In the Old and Middle Kingdoms, inscriptions were usually limited to a bare commentary on what was depicted in the reliefs. Only in the New Kingdom did sacred scriptures, magical formulae and other, more secular texts make their way on to the walls. From then on, every bit of space between reliefs was filled with text.

Magical powers

The reliefs would show the everyday cult business of the temple, such as the replenishment of the offerings altars, as well as more occasional rituals carried out by the king – or, more likely, a priest acting in his name. These secret ceremonies were meant to perpetuate the creation of the world and maintain the order created by the gods.

Inscribing its text on a temple wall heightened a ritual's power. The hieroglyphs had the power to perpetuate through eternity the performance of the rituals they described. If the cult were to fade away, the Universe would still function, thanks to the power of the texts.

▶ **The white chapel of Senusret I**
Built by the Twelfth-Dynasty pharaoh Senusret I (1965–1920 BC), this barge sanctuary in the precincts of the Amun temple at Karnak was dismantled in the middle of the New Kingdom (1550–1069 BC), and its stones used as infill on the third pylon. It was rebuilt in the twentieth century. The pharaoh stands face to face with Amun, manifest as Amun-Ra and Amun-Min, in the reliefs on its square pillars. The texts identify the king and the gods and evoke the ritual exchange between them.

❝ *Year 30, 4th month of the akhet season, day 1. The appearance of the good god in the temple of Amun … His Majesty was looking for something splendid for his father Amun-Ra, as he determined the first sed festival for his son resting on his throne and announced numerous (sed festivals) for him in Thebes.* ❞

(Jubilee inscription)

A pharaonic cartouche encloses two names: Senusret and his throne name, Kheperkara.

Amun-Ra stands before the pharaoh in this relief. The inscription, part of a rite of adoration, reads 'Praise the god four times.'

The nomes of Egypt are personified in the reliefs on the barrier walls. The accompanying texts list the name and size of each nome.

▼ Relief from Kom Ombo
Most of the reliefs at the double temple at Kom Ombo, north of Aswan, were created in the reign of Ptolemy XII Neos Dionysos (80–51 BC). The names of the pharaoh appear in cartouches guarded by the two titular gods of the temple – the falcon-headed Haroeris, an aspect of Horus, and the crocodile god Sobek.

◀ Obelisk of Thutmose III
The columns of text covering this Eighteenth-Dynasty monument tell its history. The stone was hewn from the quarries of Aswan in the reign of Thutmose III (1479–1425 BC), but he died before it was erected. It lay in a workshop in Karnak until Thutmose IV (1400–1390 BC), its originator's grandson, had his own cartouche added to it and erected the obelisk east of the temple. At just over 32m (105ft), it is the tallest obelisk ever erected in Egypt, and now stands in Rome.

The Horus name of Thutmose III is followed by a sign for 'two ladies', referring to Nekhbet and Wadjyt, the protective goddesses of Upper and Lower Egypt, respectively.

The names of Thutmose IV, who had the obelisk erected at the Karnak temple, are carved in columns on the side of the monument; those of his grandfather are in the centre.

❝ *He had it made as a monument for his father Amun, the lord of the two countries, by erecting two large obelisks for him at the front of the temple, with a pyramidion of djam gold … so that he be blessed with life like Ra in all eternity.* ❞

(Obelisk inscription)

▼ Images and text
In the temples of the New Kingdom, colourful reliefs of kings and gods engaged in rituals covered most vertical surfaces. The columns of the mortuary chapel of Rameses III at Medinet Habu provide some of the best preserved examples. On the right, Rameses offers, according to the inscription, jugs of milk. On the left, identified by name as well as their attributes, are the deities Amun-Min and Isis.

THE WRITTEN WORD

By far the most common subject for a temple relief is the king and the god standing face to face, with a short expository text identifying the occasion. The pharaoh, whose names and titles are contained in a cartouche, makes an offering to the god, to sustain him and ensure his well-being. The offering may be material or spiritual, and is often defined in the title of the scene, such as 'Consecrating the white bread' or 'Worshipping the god'.

In return for the offering, the god grants the sovereign gifts to help him in his role as ruler of Egypt: life, stability, power, health and, above all, happiness. On this exchange – which often ends with an offering of Maat, or natural harmony and balance, to nourish the god – depends the maintenance of the order created by the gods.

As well as temple ritual, the reliefs and texts provide a great deal of information about other religious occasions, such as festivals, as well as royal ceremonies including the coronation and the sed festival or jubilee, at which the king reaffirmed the legitimacy of his rule.

▶ **Making an offering**
The chambers around the inner sanctuary of a temple depicted scenes of everyday ritual. Here, at Luxor, Amenhotep III (1390–1352 BC) offers beef, including the prized foreleg, to Amun, the temple deity. Reliefs always show the pharaoh carrying out rituals, although, in reality, a high priest usually did this on his behalf.

> *Beginning of the records of the victory of the king of Upper and Lower Egypt … which he gained over the land of Khatti and Naharina, over Karkemish and the land of Qadesh.*
>
> (Report of the Battle of Qadesh)

Oval shields enclose the names of the cities conquered by the pharaoh.

Cartouches of Thutmose III are still partially visible on the ruined wall in front of the king, who wears the red crown of Lower Egypt.

Conquered cities are named on the chests of bound prisoners led to the king by the goddess of the west.

Campaign journals and king novellas

Among the more secular subjects for temple reliefs are the military exploits of the king. Each victory represents a symbolic triumph over the chaotic forces that were a constant threat to the world. Texts accompanying these reliefs are naturally more elaborate than those in offering scenes. New Kingdom pharaohs, such as the conquering Thutmose III, Sety I and his son Rameses II – or even Rameses III – used temple walls to narrate their military campaigns in some detail.

Sometimes, the inscriptions take a more literary turn. A good example is the poetic report of the Battle of Qadesh in *c.* 1274 BC, and the great victory claimed by Rameses II. Such tales about the deeds of individual rulers are usually structured in the same way; this form of composition is today described as the king novella.

▲ Naming the gods
Although gods depicted in temple reliefs can sometimes be identified by their appearance or headdress, they are always named in the inscriptions to avoid confusion. Several gods, for example, had the head of a falcon; this one is Horus, son of Isis (Harsiese). Inscriptions were also necessary to distinguish goddesses such as Hathor and Isis, who were often shown with the same robe and hairstyle.

◄ Campaign reports
The reliefs on the seventh pylon at Karnak, built by Thutmose III (1479–1425 BC), bear the image of an oversized pharaoh smiting his enemies, a traditional scene symbolizing the conquest of chaos by order. In this case, though, the texts list the conquered peoples and evoke the very real campaigns led by the pharaoh to build his empire in Syria-Palestine and the Levant.

► Unchanging style
Temple inscriptions in Ancient Egypt were always in hieroglyphs, even when the country was ruled by Persian, Greek or Roman pharaohs. Later temple inscriptions had more information than earlier ones, and the number of signs used grew from around 700 to more than 6,000. The secret of reading these texts was lost soon after the temples were closed in AD 391.

Coffin Texts

The ritual texts and magic spells known as the Coffin Texts *were used from the First Intermediate period (2181-2055 BC) until the Middle Kingdom (2055-1650 BC), allowing ordinary people the same access to funerary rites - and the afterlife - as the pharaoh.*

The *Coffin Texts* are a group of more than 1,000 spells of a religious nature, which were written in hieroglyphs or a cursive script on wooden coffins in the First Intermediate period and in the Middle Kingdom. Most of these inscribed coffins were found in necropolises in Middle and Upper Egypt.

The texts, a collection of ritual texts, hymns, prayers and magic spells, which were meant to help the deceased in his journey to the afterlife, originated from the *Pyramid Texts*, a sequence of mainly obscure spells carved on the internal walls of the pyramids of the Old Kingdom. The *Pyramid Texts* were exclusively for the king and his family, but the *Coffin Texts* were used mainly by the nobility and high-ranking officials, and by ordinary people who could afford to have them copied. The *Coffin Texts* meant that anyone, regardless of rank and with the help of various spells, could now have access to the afterlife.

▼ **Coffin of Khnumhotep**
The interior of this wooden coffin of an early Twelfth-Dynasty governor is decorated with *Coffin Texts* inscriptions, along with paintings of food offerings. The exterior is ornamented with horizontal and vertical bands of hieroglyphs, and with two wedjat eyes (eyes of Horus). These are painted on the east-facing side at the level of the head and allow the deceased to observe the world outside.

The written formulae were designed to help the deceased in his journey to the afterlife.

The coffin, made of durable wood, represented the eternal dwelling-place of the deceased.

▼ **Pyramid of Amenemhat III**
It is not known what texts were used in the coffins of the pharaohs of the Middle Kingdom (2055–1650 BC). Most of the kings of this period were buried in pyramid tombs, such as the one in Hawara of Amenemhat III (1855–1808 BC), which were looted by grave robbers not long after interment. The wooden coffins, along with their inscriptions, were burnt at the same time.

The inside of this coffin, discovered in the necropolis of the nomarchs of Asyut (one of the nomes of Upper Egypt), shows hieroglyphic extracts from the *Coffin Texts*, along with painted depictions of several everyday objects needed for survival in the afterlife. These include shields, a quiver, and a bow and arrows. Above them on a table sits an offering of two cooked ducks, complete with platters.

INSIGHT

The democratization of the afterlife

During the Old Kingdom (2686–2181 BC), only the pharaoh was guaranteed a place in the afterlife – in death, he was identified with Osiris and transformed into a god, with his journey to the afterlife facilitated by spells, such as those in the *Pyramid Texts*.

With the collapse of the Old Kingdom due to civil war and instability, the power of the provincial governors, or nomarchs, increased. They assumed some of the rituals associated with the pharaoh, among them the benefit of having funerary texts included in their burials. In this way, they, too, could have access to the afterlife, along with the pharaoh. Consequently, from the First Intermediate period (2181–2055 BC) through to the Middle Kingdom (2055–1650 BC), nomarchs such as the Twelfth-Dynasty governor of Asyut were buried in local necropolises in coffins decorated with funerary spells. Some of these were derived from the royal *Pyramid Texts*, while others were spells from different regions.

Ordinary individuals also wanted access to the afterlife, and to overcome the numerous dangers lurking in the underworld by using the same magic texts and rites. Gradually, throughout the Middle Kingdom, the use of *Coffin Texts* became more widespread.

A new feature, not found in the *Pyramid Texts*, was the use of pictorial vignettes. By the end of the Middle Kingdom, the *Coffin Texts* had fallen into disuse – to be replaced by a new guide to the afterlife, the *Book of the Dead*.

The wedjat eyes enabled the deceased to look out at the world from which he had passed, and also to see the rising sun.

The 'hetep-di-nesw' (a gift which the king gives) was a prayer asking for offerings to be brought to the deceased. It was often written on the exterior of a coffin, as here. Usually, the first line of the formula asks for the king to make gifts to the gods Osiris or Anubis; it then lists the various items of food and drink required.

The *Coffin Texts* appear not only on coffins, but also sometimes on the walls of the burial chambers and on papyrus rolls and mummy masks. They were usually written in black.

As it was impossible to write all the texts on one coffin, the owner of the tomb chose the particular extracts he wanted. Some spells were used more often than others and came to be associated with particular necropolises. High-ranking individuals of the Thebes region, for instance, used spells addressed to Osiris, while the necropolis at el-Bersha in Middle Egypt principally used texts from the *Book of Two Ways*, a sort of guide book to the underworld.

Paths through the underworld

Illustrated by a map depicting roads and canals, the text of the *Book of Two Ways* relates the journey that the deceased must take in order to arrive at the place of his rebirth. Knowledge of the spells and possession of the map meant that the deceased, like the pharaohs in times past, could negotiate the dangers of the underworld and achieve eternal life.

DOCUMENT

From the *Coffin Texts* to the *Book of the Dead*

The *Coffin Texts* were partly the inspiration for the *Book of the Dead* of the New Kingdom (1550–1069 BC), when the spells were written on papyrus rolls. Some of the formulae point to the 'negative confession of sin', which can be found in a more developed form in the *Book of the Dead*. The deceased had to deny having sinned in his life and underwent a trial before a court of gods to prove his purity and innocence. Only if his denial of sin was accepted did the deceased proceed to eternal life in the underworld.

Some coffins depict a map of the underworld with various demonic creatures. The texts accompanying this map, known as the *Book of Two Ways*, gave precise instructions about how to overcome the dangers posed by these creatures. The 'guiding' function of the *Coffin Texts* gradually became more important from the Second Intermediate period (1650–1550 BC) on and

was eventually incorporated in the *Book of the Dead*, the use of which became more widespread than that of the *Coffin Texts*.

As this 21st-Dynasty papyrus (right) shows, the texts were illustrated with vignettes.

In a funeral procession, people carry offerings and tomb furnishings for the deceased to use in the afterlife.

Illustrations and texts are rendered directly on to the wooden walls of the coffin.

The colour of the inscriptions is mostly black - as in the manuscripts written on papyri - with red headings.

Horizontal friezes between the text columns depict people with a variety of funerary offerings.

The vertical columns list the objects needed by the deceased for the afterlife.

The texts are written in cursive hieroglyphs, a style similar to but slightly different from the hieratic script.

◄ Iqer's coffin
This coffin from the late Twelfth Dynasty was found in Gebelein, south of Thebes and the site of a Middle Kingdom temple of Hathor. Only its interior has been preserved. The decoration includes horizontal friezes of figurative designs showing people with offerings, together with scenes of the burial rites. The texts between the friezes are inscribed in black.

INSIGHT

The gods of the *Coffin Texts*

The gods appearing in the *Coffin Texts* mainly belong to the group associated with creation and, in particular, with the creation myth of Heliopolis centring on the sun god Ra. Geb (the earth) and Nut (the sky), Shu (air) and Tefnut (moisture) feature prominently, along with Nephthys, Isis and Osiris, and their son Horus. The most dangerous enemy was Apophis, a giant serpent, who symbolized the forces of chaos and evil. Hathor (below, as the cow goddess with human face and cow's ears) also appears in texts from Gebelein, where she was the main deity.

Osiris, as god of the dead and the afterlife, is very often represented, and, as part of the democratization of funerary religion, the deceased himself sometimes appears as Osiris.

References to other creation myths are found in some texts. One is that of Hermopolis Magna, which attributes the creation of the world to four pairs of gods in the shape of snakes or frogs, symbolizing different aspects of the chaos before creation.

Above: The image of the kneeling Isis with raised arms as a gesture of protection is a common coffin decoration.

Left: Osiris, god of the dead, is one of the most familiar coffin motifs.

Administrative Papyri

Egypt's prosperity was founded on a stratified, centralized bureaucracy with a network of scribes throughout the country. These functionaries kept accounts and made reports on countless papyri, which provide insights into the social and economic life of Ancient Egypt.

The oldest written comments in Egypt were of a bureaucratic nature: small labels with details about the funerary equipment in the kings' tombs of the 'Zero' Dynasty (*c.* 3150–3100 BC). While scribes would make preliminary reports or notes using ostraca, pieces of stone that were later discarded, the more important administrative files were written on papyrus. These were stored in the archives of the government institutions and the temples, which had their own bureaucracies. All administrative papyri were written in cursive hieratic or (from the seventh century BC) demotic script. Hieroglyphs were too cumbersome for the needs of everyday life.

The great central repository of all this information was the office of the vizier, which collated and classified papyri concerning the stewardship and allocation of land, the level of the annual flood, the collection of taxes, the careers of bureaucrats and reports on local administration, as well as the results of judicial disputes.

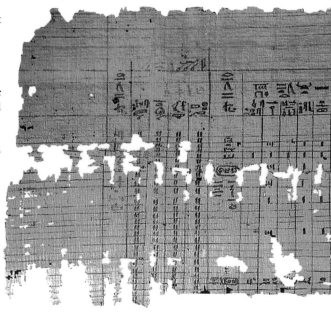

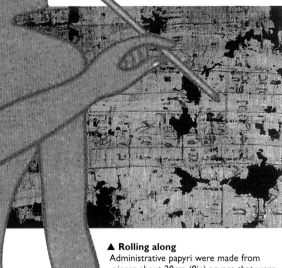

◀ **The ubiquitous scribes**
Huge numbers of scribes – rarely, if ever, separated from their palettes and brushes – were the cogs that ensured the smooth running of the government machine.

▲ **Rolling along**
Administrative papyri were made from pieces about 20cm (8in) square that were then stuck together to create a continuous roll long enough for the purpose the scribe had in mind.

▶ Early hieratic
Papyri recovered from the funerary complex of the Fifth-Dynasty pharaoh Neferirkara (2475–2455 BC) at Abusir are the earliest known documents written in hieratic script. At this stage the signs were still fairly close to the hieroglyphs from which they derived.

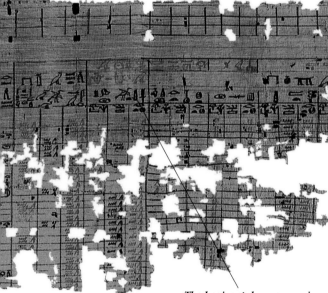

A monthly account of the offerings delivered to the funerary temple is the subject of this fragment of papyrus.

A cartouche bearing the king's name identifies the beneficiary of the offerings brought to the temple.

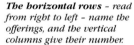

The horizontal rows - read from right to left - name the offerings, and the vertical columns give their number.

◀ The Abusir papyri
The numerous administrative papyri found in the funerary temple of Neferirkara at the necropolis of Abusir, north of Saqqara, are devoted to temple business. There are accounts of the food, unguents and fabrics offered by the temple, and texts that lay out the daily lives of the priests who worked there. These priests benefited from the solar temple built by Neferirkara at nearby Abu Roash. The custom of highlighting important passages by using red ink rather than black was already established at this stage.

◀ The temples of Abusir
Each royal pyramid in the Abusir necropolis had its own mortuary temple with a priesthood and administrators dedicated to the service of the dead king.

▲ The evolution of hieratic
This document from a temple archive at Thebes from the New Kingdom (1550–1069 BC) highlights the changes in hieratic script since the Old Kingdom.

Stelae, Books of Stone

Among the most important antiquities of Ancient Egypt, from the Old Kingdom to Roman times, stelae come in many different types, shapes and decorations.

Stelae were usually made of sandstone or harder kinds of stone such as granite or diorite, but wood was also used in later times. They were between 40cm (16in) and 4m (13ft) in height and could stand free or be built into a wall. Although generally rectangular, with either a square or rounded top, there were countless variations. The hieroglyphs and decorations were carved in sunk relief.

The function of stelae

Stelae fulfilled several functions. There were votive, commemorative and liminal, or boundary, stelae, but the largest group was the tomb stelae. These represented one of the most significant elements of Ancient Egyptian tombs. Their picture area showed the owner of the stele, often with his family, and the inscription listed the name and titles of the deceased after a prayer to one, or several, of the gods of the dead and a request for offerings. Less frequently, an autobiographical text provided additional information about the individual's life.

In the mastaba tombs of the Old Kingdom (2686–2181 BC), stelae functioned as false doors, symbolizing a passage between the present and the afterlife, which allowed the deceased to receive offerings. These were both real and represented by formulae on the false door.

◀ **Cult stele for Rameses II**
This slab belongs to a group of stelae from the Ramesside residence of Piramesse (near modern Qantir in the Delta) that attest to the cult of the deified king. In the upper register, Rameses II (1279–1213 BC) is depicted in front of his own statue offering incense; in the lower one is the donor of the stele, a military official.

Amenemhat is sitting on a stool with lion legs in front of the offerings table and ritual vases.

▶ **Tomb stele of Amenemhat**
This stele from the Middle Kingdom is decorated with depictions of the owner, Amenemhat, and his family. He was overseer of the royal carpenters, and his most important tools – an axe and a saw – can be seen in the bottom row of the picture.

The text under the arch contains the offerings formula that always starts with the words 'hetep dj njswt' - 'a gift which the king gives'.

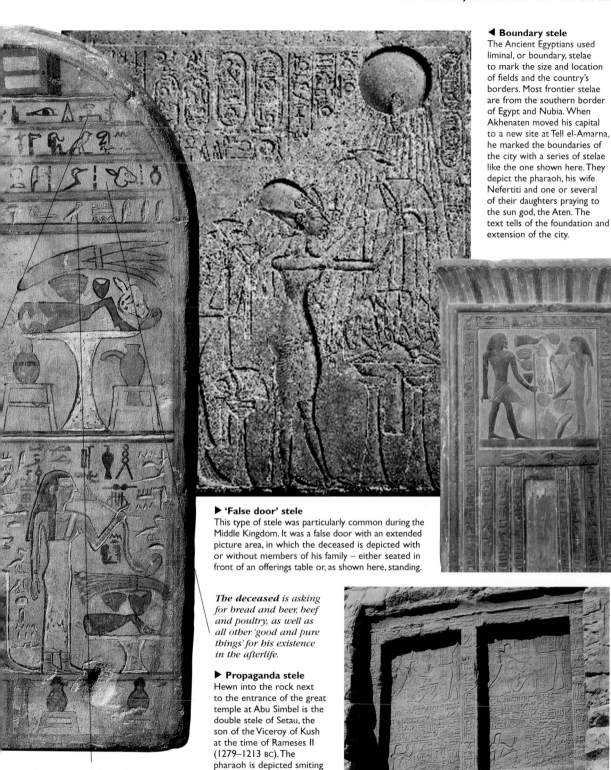

◀ **Boundary stele**
The Ancient Egyptians used liminal, or boundary, stelae to mark the size and location of fields and the country's borders. Most frontier stelae are from the southern border of Egypt and Nubia. When Akhenaten moved his capital to a new site at Tell el-Amarna, he marked the boundaries of the city with a series of stelae like the one shown here. They depict the pharaoh, his wife Nefertiti and one or several of their daughters praying to the sun god, the Aten. The text tells of the foundation and extension of the city.

▶ **'False door' stele**
This type of stele was particularly common during the Middle Kingdom. It was a false door with an extended picture area, in which the deceased is depicted with or without members of his family – either seated in front of an offerings table or, as shown here, standing.

The deceased is asking for bread and beer, beef and poultry, as well as all other 'good and pure things' for his existence in the afterlife.

▶ **Propaganda stele**
Hewn into the rock next to the entrance of the great temple at Abu Simbel is the double stele of Setau, the son of the Viceroy of Kush at the time of Rameses II (1279–1213 BC). The pharaoh is depicted smiting his enemies in front of Amun-Ra (right) and Horus (left); the lower part shows Setau himself at prayer.

The owner of the stele is not identified by his depiction, but by the name and titles listed.

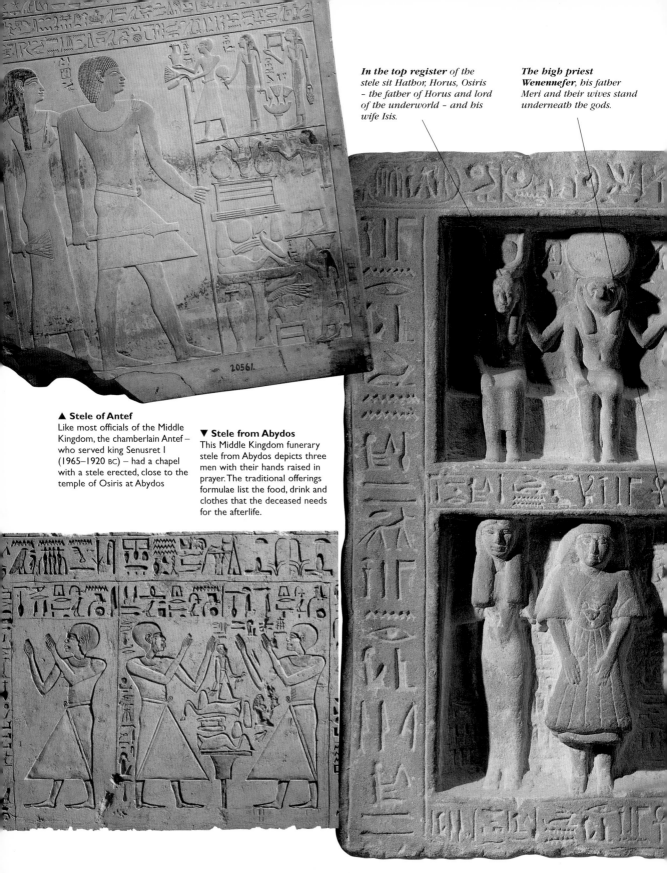

In the top register *of the stele sit Hathor, Horus, Osiris – the father of Horus and lord of the underworld – and his wife Isis.*

The high priest Wenennefer*, his father Meri and their wives stand underneath the gods.*

▲ Stele of Antef
Like most officials of the Middle Kingdom, the chamberlain Antef – who served king Senusret I (1965–1920 BC) – had a chapel with a stele erected, close to the temple of Osiris at Abydos

▼ Stele from Abydos
This Middle Kingdom funerary stele from Abydos depicts three men with their hands raised in prayer. The traditional offerings formulae list the food, drink and clothes that the deceased needs for the afterlife.

Both the throne and the birth names of the ruling king - Usermaatra Setepenra Rameses (II)-meri-Imen - are twice engraved in cartouches in this inscription.

The vertical inscriptions list the names and titles of the men - Wenennefer and Meri - who were both high priests of Osiris.

Votive stelae were exclusively erected in temples by pilgrims to pay homage to the gods or sacred animals. Their picture area showed the donor of the stele praying in front of the deity worshipped at that particular sanctuary. The workmanship of these was often fairly basic, as they were produced in large numbers by local craftsmen, who sold them to devotees.

Deeds and decrees

Commemorative stelae were placed in temples by the pharaoh, or his senior officials, detailing important events of his reign. These include the Kamose Stelae, which recount the defeat of the Hyksos, the Victory Stele describing the campaigns of the Nubian pharaoh Piy as he reconquered the country, and the Restoration Stele of Tutankhamun (1336-1327 BC) detailing the religious reforms enacted after the Amarna period. In Ptolemaic times (332-30 BC), decrees issued by the pharaoh and the priesthood were inscribed on stelae in hieroglyphs, demotic script and Greek, the most famous example of which is the Rosetta Stone.

The simplest boundary stelae marked the edges of fields, while the more sophisticated versions defined the borders of the country, particularly in the south. Uniquely, Akhenaten marked the boundaries of his new capital at Tell el-Amarna with stelae.

◄ Stele of Wenennefer

This almost square stele represents a small naos (shrine) with several figures worked in high relief. In the upper niche, the family of gods from Abydos and the goddess Hathor are sitting on a common throne. Below are four praying figures – the high priest of Osiris, Wenennefer, alongside his father, Meri, his mother and his wife.

The goddesses Hathor and Isis are both wearing the sun disc and cow's horns.

Isis, sitting next to Osiris, is identified by her name engraved next to her figure.

▲ The 'Dream' stele of Thutmose IV

Thutmose IV (1400–1390 BC) had a stele erected between the front paws of the Great Sphinx at Giza recording an event from his youth. Hunting close to the pyramids, the young prince became tired and lay down in the shadow of the Great Sphinx, who told him in a dream that he would become king on condition that he removed the sand that almost covered the monument.

◀ **Stele of Huni**
This stele shows Huni (2637–2613 BC), the last king of the Third Dynasty, being embraced by the falcon-headed Horus. This is among the oldest depictions of the god. Today, the stele is held in the Louvre Museum in Paris, but the location of its discovery remains unknown.

▲ **Tomb stele of Itjer**
Rectangular stelae such as this were popular in mastaba tombs at Giza from the Old Kingdom (2686–2181 BC). This one shows the deceased Itjer and his wife seated at an offerings table that is piled with loaves. The text lists the thousands of offerings that were made at the funeral.

▼ **Stelae at Meidum**
On the east side of the pyramid of Sneferu (2613–2589 BC) at Meidum, there is a small chapel with an altar and two high limestone stelae. Unlike the stelae of Sneferu at Dahshur, the Meidum pair has neither decoration nor inscription, as the pyramid complex was never completed.

▶ **Wooden stele**
From the Third Intermediate period (1069–747 BC) to Greco-Roman times (332 BC–AD 395), stelae were made from wood and painted plaster. This example depicts the owner of the stele and his ba praying in front of the sun barge during its journey through the underworld. In the picture area beneath, the deceased is in front of Osiris, Isis, Nephthys and Anubis. To the left are the gods Shu and Tefnut.

▼ **Stele of Hatshepsut**
This arched stele, which was formerly erected in Thebes, shows Hatshepsut (1473–1458 BC) dressed as a male pharaoh offering wine to the god Amun-Ra. Behind her stands her predecessor Thutmose III (1479–1425 BC), wearing the white crown of Upper Egypt.

▶ **Greco-Roman stele**
This tomb stele from the third century AD, today in the Egyptian Museum in Turin, bears an image of Theanous, who died at the age of 49. She is wearing the pleated robe typical of the time and holding a drinking bowl in her right hand.

The Rosetta Stone

During Napoleon Bonaparte's Egyptian campaign (1798-1801), one of his officers made a momentous discovery when he overturned a stone inscribed in three scripts, which provided the key to the deciphering of Ancient Egyptian hieroglyphs.

N apoleon's Egyptian expedition in 1798 was not merely a military one to cut off the Suez trade route to the Indies, the main source of British wealth. It also had a cultural and scientific purpose. Napoleon took with him mathematicians, economists, artists, architects, musicians and engineers to make a study of the country in every detail. In this, he was notably successful, although his military campaign was a disaster.

In British possession

Soon after landing in the country, the French fleet was destroyed by Nelson in the Battle of the Nile (1 August 1798). Three years later, the French army was defeated by the British near Alexandria and forced to hand over all the Ancient Egyptian antiquities its forces had gathered together. Among them was the Rosetta Stone, discovered in 1799 by François-Xavier Bouchard, who was an officer in Napoleon's engineering corps.

▼ **Jean-François Champollion**
In 1801, the French left Egypt with engravings of the Rosetta Stone. Using these copies, Jean-François Champollion (1790–1832) began to decipher the hieroglyphs in 1822. In 1828, as a member of a Franco-Tuscan expedition, he visited Egypt and Nubia in the company of his friend and fellow Egyptologist Ippolito Rosellini (1800–1843). In this painting of the pair in Egypt, Champollion is seated in the centre with Rosellini standing to his right.

DOCUMENT

A triscripted document

The Rosetta Stone is inscribed with a decree of 196 BC by the priests of Memphis bestowing special honours upon the pharaoh Ptolemy V Epiphanes (205–180 BC). It was for services rendered to the temples, including the reduction of taxes. The text has been reconstructed thanks to the discovery of copies of the same decree on other stelae of the same period. Written in three scripts – hieroglyphs, Demotic and Greek – the Rosetta Stone became the key to deciphering hieroglyphs.

Alphabetic signs *used to write the royal name of Ptolemy in a cartouche were the first hieroglyphs identified by Champollion.*

Greek text *features the name of Ptolemy V, which Champollion compared with the hieroglyphs in the cartouche.*

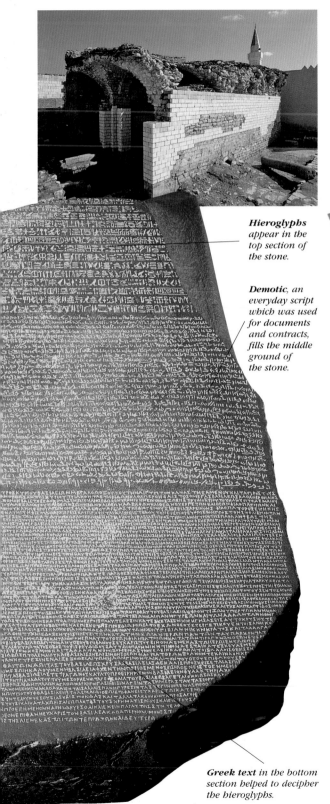

Hieroglyphs appear in the top section of the stone.

Demotic, an everyday script which was used for documents and contracts, fills the middle ground of the stone.

Greek text in the bottom section helped to decipher the hieroglyphs.

◀ **The Rosetta fortress**

Rashid, or Rosetta, a town on the Nile Delta close to Alexandria, is the site of a medieval fortress, which the French called Fort Julian. In 1799, French soldiers in the engineering corps received orders to strengthen the fortifications against a possible attack by Turkish and English troops. During the excavation work, Lieutenant François-Xavier Bouchard noticed the stone embedded in a wall. Aware of the importance of his discovery, Bouchard notified his superiors. The Rosetta Stone, one of the many antiquities seized by the British as spoils of war, is now in the British Museum in London.

▶ **The key to understanding hieroglyphs**

The Rosetta Stone is a slab of grey granitoid about 1.14m (3¾ft) high. Re-cut in Islamic times before being incorporated into the fortress wall, the stone was formerly in an open vault, surmounted by a winged disk depicting various gods.

PROFILE

Napoleon and Champollion

Napoleon Bonaparte, after being quickly informed of the Rosetta Stone's discovery, ordered engravings and copies of it to be produced. These were to be made available to the scholars of Europe. Among Champollion's most serious rivals in deciphering the hieroglyphs were an Englishman Thomas Young (1773–1829) and a Dane Johann David Akerblad (1763–1819).

However, by 1822 Champollion was the only one to understand that the hieroglyphic script (above) was not purely symbolic, but rather was based on both ideograms (pictures representing words) and phonograms (alphabetic signs).

A passionate admirer of Napoleon (right), Champollion met the emperor at Grenoble after his return from Elba and received encouragement for his work on a Coptic dictionary – the language of the early Egyptian Christians, which the young scholar had also mastered. This was eventually published following Champollion's death in 1832.

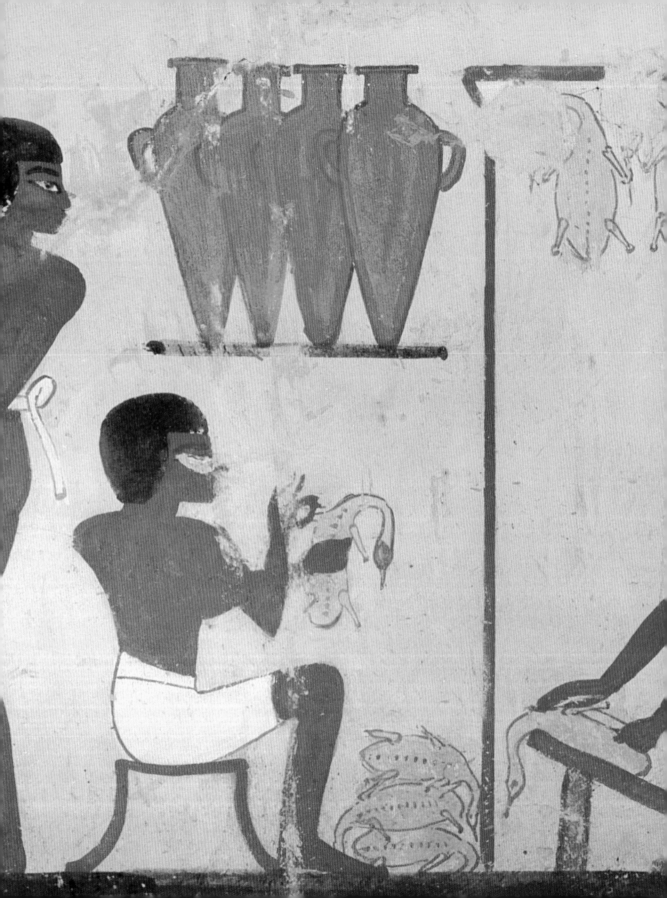

Treasures in the Home

Wall and vase paintings, as well as figurines found in tombs, show ancient Egyptians using a wide range of domestic material goods. Some were utilitarian, but nevertheless precious to their owners, while others were well crafted and beautifully decorated. Wealthy Egyptians possessed many intricately made luxury items, from makeup jars and kohl cases to fine hair combs and footbaths.

What is so breathtaking is the familiarity of household objects in both form and function. Wood-framed high-back chairs with woven seats, carved pillow rests and baskets were made with time-honoured techniques and from materials used to this day.

The heart of the home was the kitchen and the courtyard, where women ground flour in stone pestles and mortars, refined it through papyrus sieves and fermented grains in huge pitchers to make beer. These everyday objects were the backbone of domestic life, so valued that they feature in tomb statuettes and wall paintings.

Egyptian beliefs were never far away, even in the execution of chores. Everyday objects and utensils were often adorned with religious images and icons – a natural, unselfconscious decoration. Functional items such as makeup palettes became elaborately shaped and carved *objets d'art*. From the home, they made their way into tombs as grave goods, and took on a different function – one that was ceremonial rather than cerebral.

Preparing Food
A detail of a painting from the tomb of Nakht (c.1421–1413 B.C.E.) depicting the plucking and dressing of poultry after a hunt.

The Magic of Jewels

The Egyptians wore jewellery from the earliest times. Over the centuries, as the methods of working metals and stones were perfected, so the designs became more complex and sophisticated.

For the pharaoh and his dignitaries, jewellery was an indispensable part of their finery, for the colour of jewels enhanced the delicate white linen garments and heavy curled wigs worn by royal persons and members of the ruling class. Jewellery not only fulfilled a decorative function, however, but also played a magical role both for the living and the dead. Decorative symbols, such as the ankh life sign, the djed pillar of stability, the protecting udjat eye, the scarab of rebirth and images of the gods, dispensed all sorts of benefits to the owner of the object.

Materials and colours were not chosen by chance. They, too, had symbolic significance. Gold, for instance, was a divine metal, regarded as the flesh of Ra and the other gods, while lapis lazuli, which originated in Afghanistan, imitated the appearance of the heavens and was superior to all other metals, apart from gold and silver. The green of turquoise, associated with vegetation, was the emblem of youth and rebirth.

Scarab and goddesses

This detail from Tutankhamun's pectoral, or breastplate (above right), shows a winged scarab framed by the goddesses Nephthys (left) and Isis (right).

Nephthys is recognizable by the symbolic temple and basket worn on her head.

The flesh of Nephthys, a goddess associated with rebirth, is turquoise, the colour of regeneration and eternal life.

A necklace and bracelets on the arms and wrists are among the goddess's adornments.

The cloisonné technique, with inlays of coloured glass carefully cut and fitted, reproduces a net pattern on the dresses of the two goddesses.

▶ Tutankhamun's pectoral
A winged scarab sits in the centre of a shrine of which the roof has been replaced by the solar disc and the wings of the falcon Horus. Elaborately arranged uraeus serpents, with sun discs in their coils, decorate the upper corners (detailed, left).

The winged scarab, or dung beetle, framed by the goddesses Isis and Nephthys, represents the young king, who is reborn every morning like the sun, carried by the wings of Horus, god of the sky. The piece is made of gold, cornelian and coloured glass.

Pectorals first appeared in the Twelfth Dynasty and often hung from a chain or necklace. Shaped like a trapezium or a rectangle, the pectoral was usually in the form of a shrine containing decorative designs.

The Egyptians compared the birth of the dung beetle, which emerges from a ball, with the sun, symbol of life, rising over the horizon.

The seat, or throne, is a symbol of the goddess Isis, wife of Osiris and sister of Nephthys.

Gold, a divine metal that never tarnishes, symbolizes eternity.

The goddess Isis, like her sister Nephthys, wears a necklace made up of two rows of red and blue beads.

◀ The scarab and the weighing of the heart ceremony
The scarab, carved from a hard green stone, is engraved on the back with a formula from Chapter 6 of the *Book of the Dead*. This text asks the heart not to betray the deceased during the weighing of the heart, or judgement, held in the court of Osiris.

Cosmetics & Perfumes

For the Ancient Egyptians, cosmetics and perfumes were not merely for personal adornment – they were associated with the gods and rebirth in the afterlife.

Perfumes were used in Ancient Egypt from the earliest times. Although scented oils and unguents (ointments) were most common, essences extracted by pressing flowers, such as the lily, were also used. Perfumes were originally made for religious rituals, using a wide range of aromatic plants. They were generally produced in the temples, which had their own specialist 'laboratories', making different types of incense and fragrant pastes. Many of the recipes survive and, although some of the ingredients are unknown today, they show that the Egyptians loved sweet, spicy perfumes that filled the air with their heady, long-lasting aroma.

The scent of the gods

Kyphi, the most celebrated Egyptian perfume, was burnt daily in the temple as an incense. Its ingredients included resins, such as frankincense, myrrh, mastic and pine resin; herbs and spices, such as cinnamon, cardamom, saffron, juniper, mint and the patchouli-like spikenard; along with raisins and honey. The burning and offering of incense was a means of communication with the gods, and there are many depictions of pharaohs making such fragrant offerings.

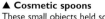

▲ Cosmetic spoons
These small objects held scented unguents for the immediate use of the owner, and were presumably scooped from a larger container.

▶ Unguent pots
The use of cosmetics dates back to early history. Cosmetics and unguents were held in high regard even in Predynastic times, proof of which are these small vessels of hardstone, found in the tombs of the Predynastic Naqada period (4000–3100 BC) and now in the Louvre in Paris.

A female servant hands a small perfume flaçon to her mistress, and fans the air to diffuse the perfume's scent.

The fan is made of ostrich plumes.

The princess's favourite dog, seated beneath her chair, adds a whimsical touch to the scene.

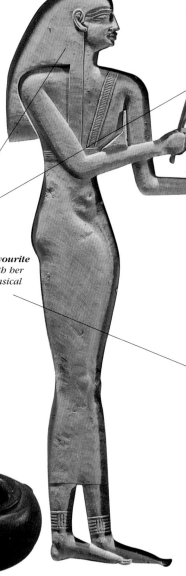

▼ The power of perfume

This tomb relief depicts Ashait, a princess of the Middle Kingdom, seated on a bench decorated with the head and the claws of a lion. The Egyptians believed that perfume was a gift of the gods, and it was used in temple ceremonies as well as for personal allure. Its links with sexuality and rebirth made it especially important in the afterlife, and many unguent jars and perfume bottles are found among tomb goods.

▶ Decorative hand mirror

This mirror, which dates from the Old Kingdom (2686–2181 BC), is made of polished bronze and decorated with the figures of Nephthys and Osiris. Its handle was possibly made of wood, metal, faience or ivory, perhaps in the shape of a papyrus stem or human figure.

The sphere-shaped bottle contained perfume or fragrant oils to be used both on the body and for scenting the princess's chamber.

The powerful, hyacinth-like scent of the lotus flower had sexual connotations, and by extension the lotus was a symbol of rebirth in the afterlife - hence its frequent depiction in tomb paintings and reliefs.

▼ Double kohl case

This double cylindrical case, made of wood and ivory, has two compartments with hinged lids for the kohl, and a slot at the back for the kohl stick.

▼ Kohl case

This charming wooden kohl case, with a geometric pattern around the base, is in the form of a palm tree. It was found in a New Kingdom tomb.

TREASURES IN THE HOME

During the New Kingdom (1550–1069 BC), perfume began to be used in beauty preparations and for personal adornment, as well as in religious rituals. Fragrant oils and unguents protected the skin in a country where the sun was extremely hot, although few but the rich could afford the exotic scents that now included imported luxuries, such as spicy green galbanum from Persia or rose-scented camel grass from Libya. Then, as now, perfumes were associated with sexuality, and in the divine scheme of things were symbols of rebirth in the afterlife.

Cosmetics – the art of beauty

Cosmetics were already in use in Predynastic times; many cosmetic spoons and make-up palettes date from this period. In Ancient Egypt, the focus was on the eyes, which were outlined with green or black eye paint to emphasize their size and shape. The ground pigments of green malachite, mixed with water to form as paste, were used until the middle of the Old Kingdom (2686–2181 BC), but were then replaced by black kohl, produced from the mineral galena, which came from the mountain regions of Sinai. Significantly, kohl had therapeutic value in protecting the eyes from infections caused by sunlight, dust or flies.

▲ Kohl container
The holes in the top of this vessel contained kohl and the sticks (introduced during the Middle Kingdom) with which to apply it. The monkeys that decorate the container hold the hieroglyph for 'protection', a reminder of kohl's role in preventing eye infections.

▼ Jar in the form of Bes
Many cosmetics containers were in the shape of figures or animals. This faience unguent jar from the Eighteenth Dynasty (1550–1295 BC) represents the dwarf god Bes, who was associated with women, childbirth and sexuality. He is therefore an appropriate image for a container which held a beauty aid to enhance appearance and sexual allure.

▶ Unguent jars
Containers for unguents and perfumed oils came in various shapes and sizes. Some were made of precious materials, such as glass or alabaster, while blue faience was a more commonplace alternative, as here.

◀ Cosmetic palette
Palettes were used to grind pigments such as malachite or galena, from which, respectively, green and kohl eye paints were made. This one is shield-shaped, with two birds' heads at the top. Their use dates from the Predynastic period (5500–3100 BC), during which time they also acquired ceremonial or magical properties; many were found as grave goods in cemeteries dating back to about 4000 BC.

▼ Mummy mask from the Roman period (30 BC–AD 395)
The mummy, or funerary, mask was first used in the First Intermediate period (2181–2055 BC) to help with the identification of the linen-wrapped mummy. This example from the Roman period has the outlined eyes and emphatic brows that were characteristic of the Egyptian style, but the features are more life-like and less stylized than on traditional Ancient Egyptian masks.

Fine brush strokes simulate the hair of these thick eyebrows. Black eye paint was often used on eyebrows to emphasize them.

Kohl was used to colour the eyelids and make the eyes appear larger. It also protected the eyes against infections.

Lip tint was used by the Romans in Egypt, but wall paintings, mummy masks and painted reliefs show little evidence of its use in pharaonic times.

Mummy masks from the Roman period show portrait-like features in the classical style rather than the idealized images that feature on earlier examples.

Clothes and Fashion

Although styles differed for men and women, Ancient Egyptian clothes were generally practical and simple, until the New Kingdom, when men's and women's fashion broke from its rather austere past and became more elegant and refined.

The typical male dress in Ancient Egypt was the loincloth. During the Old Kingdom (2686–2181 BC) and much of the Middle Kingdom (2055–1650 BC), this was a piece of rectangular fabric covering the loins and falling to just above the knee, tied around the waist with a strip of fabric or leather. Only by their jewellery could men from the wealthy classes be distinguished from farmers and artisans.

New Kingdom fashions

It was not until the New Kingdom (1550–1069 BC) that dress became more sophisticated: an apron-like arrangement was often added to the front of the loincloth, and ankle-length skirts and short-sleeved tunics began to be worn over the short loincloth. The full-length robe also made an appearance at this time. This garment had a wide neck and wide sleeves and was gathered at the waist. It is likely that developing relations with other Mediterranean countries played an important role in these new fashion trends.

▶ **Dress of a Twentieth-Dynasty prince**
In this illustration, the son of Rameses III (1184–1153 BC) wears royal garments similar to those of his father. His wide-sleeved tunic of white linen fits over a long, white loincloth, from which hangs a blue and ochre belt.

▼ **The triangular apron**
This garment, worn only by the pharaoh, consists of a loincloth and triangular apron. The end of the coloured sash is decorated with sacred cobras.

▼ **The royal schendyt**
Only the king could attach a lion's tail, symbol of strength, to his short, narrow loincloth, known as a schendyt.

▶ **Fashion in the Amarna period**
This torso is thought to represent Nefertiti, the wife of the pharaoh Akhenaten (1352–1336 BC). She wears a finely pleated linen garment, knotted under the breasts and leaving the right arm exposed. In the art style typical of the Amarna period, the transparency of the fabric serves to emphasize the body's contours, and its rounded buttocks and thighs.

The richly decorated diadem has a side flap, similar to the sidelock of youth, which indicates that the wearer is a child.

The white tunic covers only the upper arms. The wrists are adorned with costly bracelets of gold and semi-precious stones.

The loincloth is held in place by a wide belt or sash.

▼ **Karomama, queen and priestess**
In this superb bronze and gilded statuette from the Twenty-Second Dynasty (945–715 BC), Karomama, wife of Takelot II (850–825 BC), wears a decorative collar over a long, finely pleated gown with wide, winged sleeves.

▼ **Ahmose Nefertari (1570–1505 BC)**
This queen follows New Kingdom fashions, with her wide collar, winged sleeves and a high-waisted gown knotted with a jewel-encrusted, coloured sash.

▼ **A ritual garment**
Priests and kings often wore a leopard skin when performing religious rituals and on some ceremonial occasions.

▼ **Male fashion in the New Kingdom**
Fashionable wear in the New Kingdom included the short loincloth topped by a long robe of transparent, pleated linen, with a coloured sash.

INSIGHT

Royal dress

During the Old Kingdom (2686–2181 BC), the simple, short loincloth featured among a king's ceremonial garments. However, by the Middle Kingdom (2055–1650 BC), fashions had changed and more elaborate clothes were worn by the ruling classes. One of the innovations at this time was the starched, triangular apron, which

formed a flap in front of either the short or long loincloth. This was held in place by a coloured, decorative sash. More radical changes took place during the New Kingdom (1550–1069 BC), with the addition of robes and chemises, as well as variable loincloth designs. In the Greco-Roman period (332 BC–AD 395), fashion saw a 'retro' movement and the triangular apron reappeared, decorated, as in this example (above), by the familiar motif of the pharaoh triumphing over his enemies.

Women's fashions

Until the end of the Middle Kingdom, women wore a simple, long sheath dress with one or two broad shoulder straps. A transparent, long-sleeved tunic was sometimes worn over these figure-hugging dresses, as was a sort of decorative mesh tunic.

Women's clothes, along with men's, changed during the New Kingdom. Garments became looser and more sophisticated, and women wore dresses that knotted beneath their breasts and fell away more fully to their feet. Linen became increasingly fine and more highly worked, while draped and pleated effects created some very elaborate fashions. Long sleeves, for example, were often finely pleated and starched to resemble birds' wings. Most of these loose-fitting garments covered the breasts (often bared in earlier times) and the left arm, while the right arm remained exposed.

▶ **Festive garments**
Noblewomen and others of high rank dressed in all their finery on special occasions and for festive banquets, as this wall painting shows.

INSIGHT

Workmen's fashion

Unlike officials, artisans and farmers dressed in plain, inexpensive robes of different fabrics. Before linen came into use, men wore loincloths of reed or palm fibres, leather or fur with broad sashes. Shepherds, ferrymen and fishermen mainly made do with a simple leather sash from which hung a curtain of reeds; many also worked completely naked, at least until the Middle Kingdom – during this time it became rare to see an unclothed worker. Female millers, bakers and harvest workers are often depicted in a long wraparound skirt but with the upper part of the body bared.

The clothes worn by the servants of officials and dignitaries were more refined than those of simple folk. A servant depicted in an Eigteenth-Dynasty tomb (left) wears a finely pleated linen tunic and loincloth with a wide, pleated sash.

◀ The linen sheath

This detail from a Middle Kingdom stele shows the typical Egyptian dress of the time – a long, close-fitting linen sheath, supported by straps that reached from below the breasts to just above the ankles. This woman also wears a long wig, and jewellery in the form of a broad collar, bracelets, anklets and toe rings.

▼ A vizier's attire

This bronze statuette depicts a vizier of the Middle Kingdom. His distinctive garment was a long, starched robe that hung from the chest to just above the feet; it was fastened at the back with a cord. In this example, the garment is pleated in broad horizontal bands.

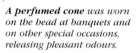

A perfumed cone was worn on the head at banquets and on other special occasions, releasing pleasant odours.

A long, thick wig of tight curls was adorned with an elaborate headdress.

The full-length festive robe of fine linen was knotted above the waist with a cord.

Sumptuous jewellery included bracelets of faience, gold and colourful semi-precious stones, along with large, heavy earrings.

A bouquet of lotus blooms and a single lotus flower across the arm complete the ensemble.

▲ Priestly garments

When carrying out their priestly duties, temple officials often wore the skin of a leopard draped over their shoulder. This dress was initially reserved for the sem priests, who played an important role in regal and private funerary rites and who were responsible for performing the 'opening of the mouth' ritual. In this stele, which dates from the Fourth Dynasty (2613–2494 BC), the priest sits in front of an offerings table.

▶ Pleated tunic

This pleated, linen tunic belonged to Nakht, a chancellor of Egypt during the Middle Kingdom. It was found in his tomb in Asyut, and is now held in the Louvre Museum, Paris.

Hygiene and Body Care

In Egypt, sweltering heat and sanitary problems often coexisted. People went to great lengths to remove dirt from their person and their life. The daily routines included cleansing the skin and mouth, grooming the hair and cleaning the finger and toe nails.

In the ruins of the palace of Rameses III (1184-1153 BC) at Medinet Habu, in the villas of the elite at Amarna, even in the dwellings of the middle classes – chief craftsmen, officials and intermediate priests – archaeologists have discovered bathrooms (or more precisely washrooms) with mud-brick walls protected from the water by slabs of limestone. Egyptians did not take baths. Instead, they poured water from a jug with a spout over their head and body – or, more likely, had a servant do it for them. Sometimes the water – which was never heated – was tipped through a vessel with holes in it, an early precursor of the showerhead. The floor sloped slightly for dirty water to drain away. The sort of homes that had bathrooms would also have had a small room set aside as a lavatory, with a pierced limestone or wood seat raised on some mud bricks, and an earthenware pot half filled with sand beneath.

The houses of the lower classes, by contrast, had no sanitary arrangements at all, and there is no archaeological evidence of public baths in pharaonic times. This does not mean that the general population did not wash – the sheer number of toilet articles that survive from Ancient Egypt testifies to the importance placed on cleanliness and grooming – but that they did so outdoors, either bathing in the Nile or sprinkling water on their face, hands and body from a small bowl and rubbing away any dirt. Water for washing was carried home by women from the river or local wells in big earthenware jars.

▼ Oils and unguents

Ointments based on fats and oils from both plant and animal sources were an important part of body care in Ancient Egypt. There was no soap. Bathers used fats mixed with chalk and limestone dust instead. Other ointments refreshed the skin in Egypt's drying climate, while oil-based fragrances were used to scent the skin. They were kept in precious pots and jars; those depicted here being carried by servants would have been reserved for sacred oils.

Tall, conical pots sealed with flat lids supplemented the smaller, rounded containers. They were used to store fragrant moisturizing oils.

▼ Personal service

Rich Egyptians were surrounded with servants who helped them with their toilette. This young woman carries an unguent pot in her left hand and a mirror in a case in her right.

◄ Jug and basin

Every household had a washing set, used particularly for sluicing the hands before and after meals. This example – comprising a tall, bucket-shaped bowl and a pot with a long, down-curved spout – is from the First Intermediate period (2181–2055 BC) tomb of Iti at Gebelein. These items are bronze, but clay and stone vessels were also used. Ritual cleansing remained important in the afterlife. Funerary stelae and tomb reliefs and paintings have depicted washing sets just like this – in use in ritual or placed close by the offerings table – throughout Egypt's history.

▶ **Feet of clay**
Divided, rectangular earthenware basins such as this, with sloping walls and the sole of a foot depicted on the central divider, are occasionally found in tombs, or carved on the walls. They may have been used for ritually cleansing or anointing the feet before entering a sacred area; water or oil would be poured over a foot placed on the rest. Feet also received non-ritual attention in Ancient Egypt. Pedicures – and manicures – are depicted in the tomb of a high-ranking Old Kingdom official, Ptahhotep.

◀ **Foot relief**
The Fourth-Dynasty mastaba tomb of Prince Rahotep has a relief that seems to show (from above) a basin like that on the right, but with two foot-rests rather than one, topped by a conical vessel (from front-on). This can be seen as a bucket of water for washing the feet or a pot of oil for anointing them.

Scented sacred oils were liberally used to perfume the celebrants of cult rituals and were offered in libations to the gods and the dead alike.

The young women carrying the oil jars are the servants of a daughter of Mentuhotep II (2004–1992 BC). This relief is carved on her sarcophagus.

INSIGHT

Ritual ablutions

Only the pharaoh and his representatives, the priests, were allowed inside Egyptian temples. Before they entered the sanctuary to perform their duties, both ruler and priests had to go through a cleansing ritual, as nothing from the profane world was supposed to enter the sanctuary. According to the Greek historian Herodotus, writing in the fifth century BC, 'the priests shaved their whole body every third day so that they had no louse or other pest when serving the gods … They wash twice a day and twice a night.' The antiquity of the practice is demonstrated by the ceremonial palette of Narmer, founder of the First Dynasty around 3100 BC. It shows a servant carrying the king's sandals and a water jug for a ritual cleansing (left) before the king enters the temple of Horus to make an offering.

A pleasant fragrance was as important as cleanliness. Scented oils were popular gifts, while lozenges made from myrrh, juniper berries, honey, incense and other ingredients sweetened the breath. Cosmetics were generally applied after bathing. All of these enhanced the appearance, but some of them had a practical use. Eye make-up – green malachite-based pigments used early in the Old Kingdom were later replaced by black kohl, based on galena – made the eyes appear bigger, but also acted as a natural disinfectant, warding off infections, and provided protection from the dazzle and glare of the Egyptian sun.

Household rubbish

The Egyptians dealt with their domestic refuse much as we do today, either burying it in waste ground or piling it up into tips. Some was dumped in waterways. The tips could be quite large – the one associated with the royal palace of Akhenaten was some 200m by 120m (650ft by 400ft) – and can be treasure troves for archaeologists; a refuse ditch dug close by the village of Deir el-Medina yielded literally thousands of ostraca that provide great insights into the everyday lives of the workmen who lived there.

A 'kulkhur' (kohl) container sits alongside a pair of sandals and a mirror beneath the woman's chair.

◄ Looking good
Mirrors were indispensable to the perfect application of make-up. The reflective surface was always a highly polished metal — copper, bronze or silver — disc. Some handles were plain, but most were decorated. They were commonly carved or moulded as a papyrus plant, the fiercely protective god Bes or a naked young woman.

▼ Bowls
These two small bowls – one of Egyptian faience and the other of calcite alabaster – were probably used for hand-washing after a meal, but it is possible they were intended as drinking vessels. Found in the tomb of an official, they are today on display at the Fitzwilliam Museum in Cambridge.

◄ Eye make-up
Egyptians – both men and women – regularly applied 'kulkhur,' or kohl, eye make-up that had a practical as well as cosmetic use, and was kept in small, rounded pots.

► Toiletries for the afterlife
Like anything else that the Ancient Egyptians found useful in life, toiletries and cosmetics were considered to be equally essential for the dead, and they formed an important part of the grave goods of wealthy people. Small containers of wood or basketwork served to store everyday toiletries, while most tombs contained 'kulkhur' vessels of various kinds of stone, glass and faience, along with combs, hairpins, copper and bronze tweezers, razor knives and small whetstones. Cosmetic articles are usually found alongside amulets in the shape of scarabs, which serve to protect health in this life and guarantee rebirth in the next.

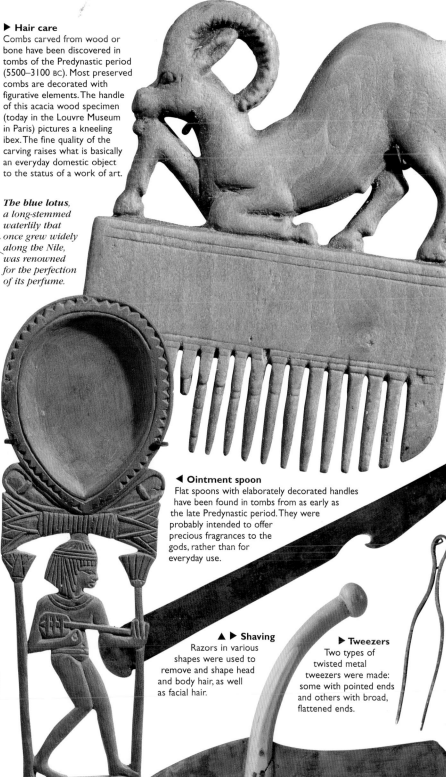

▶ **Hair care**
Combs carved from wood or bone have been discovered in tombs of the Predynastic period (5500–3100 BC). Most preserved combs are decorated with figurative elements. The handle of this acacia wood specimen (today in the Louvre Museum in Paris) pictures a kneeling ibex. The fine quality of the carving raises what is basically an everyday domestic object to the status of a work of art.

The blue lotus,
a long-stemmed
waterlily that
once grew widely
along the Nile,
was renowned
for the perfection
of its perfume.

A hunting dog similar to a modern-day greyhound sits by its master's chair.

▲ **Pleasant scents**
This tomb relief shows a couple enjoying the fragrance of blue lotus flowers, a much-prized scent in Ancient Egypt. The plant owed its popularity both to its heady, even psychotropic perfume and to its status as a symbol of regeneration and rebirth, with the flowers closing each evening to be reborn the following morning with the sun.

◀ **Ointment spoon**
Flat spoons with elaborately decorated handles have been found in tombs from as early as the late Predynastic period. They were probably intended to offer precious fragrances to the gods, rather than for everyday use.

▲ ▶ **Shaving**
Razors in various shapes were used to remove and shape head and body hair, as well as facial hair.

▶ **Tweezers**
Two types of twisted metal tweezers were made: some with pointed ends and others with broad, flattened ends.

Measuring Time

Amazingly simple devices were used in Ancient Egypt for the measurement of time. Surviving water and sun clocks show that only a very inexact determination of day and night times was possible.

The Ancient Egyptian year had 360 days and was divided into 12 months of 30 days each, as well as into 36 months each containing 10 days. At the year's end, five days remained which were considered to be 'outside' of the year, and the birthdays of Osiris, Isis, Horus, Seth and Nepthys. Each year was a quarter day shorter than the solar year, so an extra day was added every fourth year to compensate for this.

Day and night

Day and night were each divided into 12 'hours', whose length varied according to the season. From the New Kingdom (1550–1069 BC), daylight hours were measured by a sundial (setshat) of which there were two varieties: one involved measuring the length of a shadow and finding its value on a corresponding table; the other measured the progress of a shadow against an inscribed scale.

The night hours were measured from the New Kingdom onwards with a water clock (clepsydra), which was invented by the astronomer Amenemhat 'for the glory of King Amenhotep I'. This equated the passage of time with the amount of water that ran out of a hole in the base of a container.

◀ The water clock
The water clock was generally used to measure the passage of the night hours. This stone container tapers towards the bottom, where there is a small opening, often decorated with a figure of Thoth. The interior of a water clock was inscribed with 12 rings, each representing the passing of an hour. The outer surface was frequently decorated with pictures of the deities of heavenly bodies.

◀ The sundial
This pylon-shaped sundial worked by reading the sun's shadow against the 12 inscribed divisions. A small rod was placed in the hole, with the position of its shadow giving an approximation of the time of day. It is impossible to say whether such devices were actually used, or whether they served only as a model or as a votive offering.

Sety I raises his hand in a gesture of worship and presents the daughter of the sun god with a water clock.

A baboon sitting on the water clock is one of the manifestations of Thoth, god of time.

The clepsydra measured the passage of time by the depth of the water that slowly ran out of a hole in the base.

◀ Portable sundial
To measure the daylight hours, portable sundials were used, which could be placed anywhere. This simple device was positioned in an east–west orientation, with the plumb-line showing its vertical alignment. On the front surface the king is portrayed before the sun god Ra-Horakhty. This part of the device casts the sun's shadow over the surface, which is divided into one-hour segments, allowing for easy reading of the time of day.

The ibis-beaded Thoth, the moon god and lord of measurement, was thought by the Ancient Egyptians to be the inventor of all sciences.

The goddess Weret-Hekaw receives the offering from Sety I.

◀ The offering of a clepsydra
This relief is from the Temple of Amun at Karnak. Pharaoh Sety I (1294–1279 BC) kneels before the lion-headed goddess Weret-Hekaw, who receives the offering of the water clock.

▼ Sundial with a figure of Thoth
This sundial is a fixed measuring device. The part casting the sun's shadow is the small vertical slab, with Thoth, the lord of measurement in his manifestation as a baboon, sitting in front of the slab. In this type of measuring device, the shadow hit the slanted area of the block behind, which usually had one-hour segments painted onto it.

The Egyptian Calendar

Like all primitive peoples, the early Egyptians measured time by observing lunar months of 29 to 30 days, but around 2900 BC they developed the first calendar not dependent on the movements of the moon.

The first Egyptian calendars combined observations of the moon with the annual cycle of the Nile. The latter was measured with nilometers – reeds with notches cut in them to calibrate the height of the waters. Thus the Egyptian year of 12 months, each 30 days long, was divided into three four-month seasons: *akhet* ('inundation', mid-July to mid-November); *peret* ('emergence', mid-November to mid-March); and *shemu* (perhaps 'low water', the period of harvest from mid-March to mid-July). Each month comprised three 'weeks' of 10 days ('decades'), and each day was divided into 24 hours (12 daytime, 12 night-time).

The Egyptian year was extended to 365 days – the solar year – by the addition of five days following the end of *shemu*. These were regarded as the birthdays of the gods Osiris, Horus and Seth, and the goddesses Isis and Nephthys.

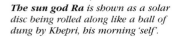

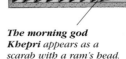

The morning god Khepri appears as a scarab with a ram's head.

The sun god Ra is shown as a solar disc being rolled along like a ball of dung by Khepri, his morning 'self'.

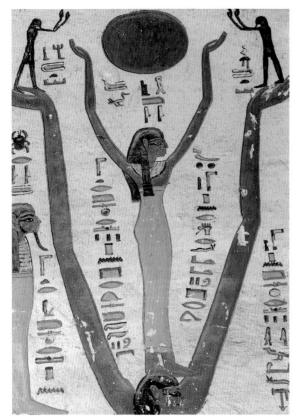

◀ **The sky goddess**
In the evening, the sky goddess Nut, who is arched above the earth and presides over the movement of the stars and the passing of time, swallows the solar disc, representing the sun god Ra. This passes through her body during the night, and she returns it to the world at dawn by 'giving birth' to Ra.

▶ **A religious calendar**
The ceiling of the hypostyle hall in the temple of Esna, built between the first and third centuries AD, is decorated with astronomical scenes. A calendar shows the dates of religious feasts, some of which match the dates of the agricultural cycle. Others, like the Feast of Opet at Thebes, were associated with particular deities.

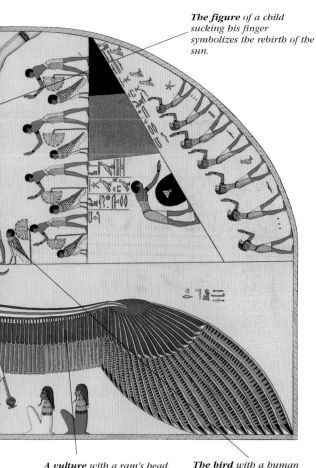

The figure of a child sucking his finger symbolizes the rebirth of the sun.

A vulture with a ram's head, possibly the goddess Nekhbet, dominates the image.

The bird with a human head represents ba, the soul of the deceased.

◀ **The morning sun**

The Egyptians gave each image of the sun a different name. In the morning, when it rose after travelling through the body of Nut, it had the appearance of a scarab beetle pushing the solar disc, and was called Khepri; in the evening, when it set, it took on the appearance of an old man, and was known as Atum.

INSIGHT

The Dendera zodiac

The picture below is a reproduction of a stela from a ceiling in the temple of Hathor, another sky goddess, at Dendera. Sculpted in relief and dating from 50 BC, the sandstone monument is now in the Louvre, Paris.

The slab shows a zodiac of a celestial sphere travelled by the stars and planets and divided into 12 equal sections. Invented by the Babylonians in the fifth century BC, and then taken up by the Greeks, the zodiac appeared in Egypt only at the end of the third century BC.

The figures around the edge of the circle represent the 36 10-day periods, or 'decades'. Above their heads are the 12 signs of the zodiac, including Pisces and Taurus, as well as the constellations known to the Egyptians.

The first depiction of the zodiacal signs, with the 10-day periods, was on the astronomical ceiling of the tomb of Senenmut, chief steward to Queen Hatsheput, at Deir el-Bahri (1463 BC). Zodiac reliefs similar to the Dendera zodiac were commonly engraved in temples and on sarcophagus lids during Greco-Roman times.

The Nile calendar

The Egyptian calendar, based originally on the annual cycle of the River Nile, had three seasons of four lunar months:

akhet: the flood season
thoth: 19 July – 17 August
paophi: 18 August – 16 September
athyr: 17 September – 16 October
sholiak: 17 October – 15 November

peret: the growing season
tybi: 16 November – 15 December
meshir: 16 December – 14 January
phamenoth: 15 January – 13 February
pharmouthi: 14 February – 15 March

shemu: the harvest season
pashons: 16 March – 14 April
payni: 15 April – 14 May
epiphi: 15 May – 13 June
mesori: 14 June – 13 July

plus five extra 'epagomenal' holy birthdays:
14 July: Osiris; 15 July: Horus; 16 July: Seth; 17 July: Isis;
18 July: Nephthys

The night sky

This drawing by Ippolito Rosellini replicates part of the ceiling of the funeral chamber of Sety I (1294–1279 BC) in the Valley of the Kings. The constellations and divisions of the sky are represented as mythological divinities. In the top part of the drawing, the constellations are aligned and by observing their positions the Ancient Egyptians determined the duration of the hours of the night. Various constellations associated with the 10-day periods, or 'decades', are depicted at the bottom.

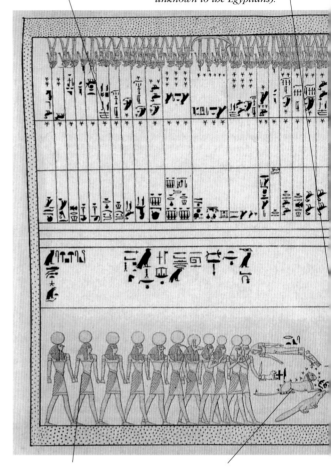

The night hours are shown at the top.

A human figure with arms spread wide possibly represents the Swan constellation (although swans were unknown to the Egyptians).

Deities flank the northern constellations in the lower half.

The Lion constellation is easily identified.

▶ **Day and night**
The ceiling of the sarcophagus room in the tomb of Rameses VI (1143–1136 BC) is decorated with pictures and inscriptions taken from the *Book of the Day* and the *Book of the Night*. These texts relate the nocturnal travels of the solar disc, representing the sun god Ra, through the body of the sky goddess Nut.

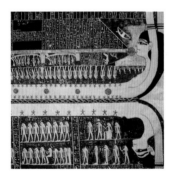

▲ **The march of time**
While births and deaths were dated by the reigns of the pharaohs, the peasants of Ancient Egypt based their yearly calendar on the flow of the Nile. Today, however, the flow of the river and its annual cycle is carefully controlled by the Aswan Dam.

The bull represents the Great Bear constellation.

*The **hippopotamus*** *carrying a crocodile is a complex representation of the Dragon constellation.*

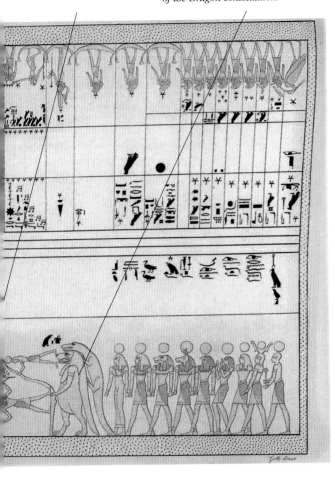

▲ **The astronomical ceiling of Senenmut**
This painting from the ceiling of the tomb of Senenmut, Queen Hatshepsut's favourite courtier – and possibly her lover, according to some Egyptologists – shows the first astronomical ceiling in Ancient Egypt. By studying the position of the stars, it has been possible to date the ceiling accurately to 1463 BC.

The picture indicates the position of the constellations visible over the different months of the year, the 12 circles with their spokes symbolizing the 12 months. Star charts, it was believed, enabled the deceased to tell the time of night or the date in the solar year.

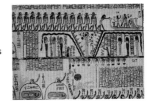

▲ **The solar clock, c. 1500 BC**
The time between the first and last hours of the day was measured by a gnomon. When the front of the gnomon is directed to the sun, its shadow is projected onto the back of the instrument. The accurate time is determined by both the length and direction of the shadow.

▼ **The sun's night voyage**
The reproductions from the *Book of the Earth* which decorate the walls of the funeral chamber in the tomb of Rameses VI (1143–1136 BC) show the gods Ra and Osiris, associated with the rebirth of the dead, and 12 women, personifying the 12 hours of the night.

The missing link

The birthdays of the five gods (born only through the intervention of Thoth, the god of knowledge, who provided five extra days of light), took the Egyptian year back to its beginning – 19 July on our Gregorian calendar. This was the date of the rising of Sirius, the brightest star in the sky, which was personified by the star-crowned goddess Sopdet. Surviving textual accounts of this event (and its observation) form the basis of the traditional chronology of Egypt.

However, there remained a discrepancy between the civil year and its divisions – which gave the Egyptians a reasonably accurate means of measuring time – and the solar year, which was six hours longer. In effect, the difference meant that the civil year and the seasonal year coincided precisely just once every 1,460 years. This hardly bothered most Egyptians, and it was not corrected until the Ptolemaic period, when the notion of a 'leap year' (one extra day every fourth year) was introduced by Ptolemy III, dating the New Year from 29 August.

▼ **The Aztec calendar**
Located in the National Museum of Anthropology in Mexico City, Mexico, the famous sun stone or Aztec calendar offers a Mesoamerican explanation for the origins and early history of the world. The centre of the umbo or boss is occupied by Tonatiuh, the sun god. The four rectangles surrounding him evoke the four eras experienced by humanity during its history.

In the central circle are the gods corresponding to the 20 days of the Aztec month, while the two snakes in the outer circle symbolize the celestial dome. The Aztecs believed that the sun required blood for fuel and, according to some Spanish chroniclers, between 20,000 and 50,000 people a month were sacrificed in order to placate it.

Private Temples, Public Pageants

Ancient Egypt's artistic development arose from a set of beliefs and influences that hinged on gratitude for the Nile's rich, seasonal waters, and anxiety that they might fail, bringing famine and chaos. Many of ancient Egypt's treasures reflect the people's fervour and fear – and their dependency on god-like kings and queens. It was perceived that it was these kings and queens who decided whether the granaries were empty or full.

Beautifully crafted stone and metalwork statues of gods show an elaborate pantheon of human and animal forms – sometimes fused into one body. Some gods expressed themselves through two conjoined animal forms, although at times these same gods would be represented separately. There were even gods who took care of and guarded each other, and their statutes can often be found together.

But the Egyptian masses were involved neither in temple culture nor the priesthood, which was the preserve of the wealthy. The poor did take part in street festivals to honour their deities, probably out of reverence, fear and possibly a bit of opportunistic revelry. At these times, treasured statues of the gods were paraded for all to see, and then taken back home to their temples. Here, in the enclosed temple grounds, priests tended to their every whim – even growing food to offer them.

Pharaoh in the Underworld
A wall painting of Tutankhamun accompanied by Anubis and Nephthys. Jackal-headed Anubis was the guardian of the dead, who greeted the souls in the Underworld. It was he who deemed the deceased worthy of becoming a star. Nephthys was considered to be the nurse of the Pharaoh himself.

The Gods of Egypt

The Ancient Egyptians worshipped a number of gods and goddesses, each of whom had different roles or functions, as well as a variety of creation myths.

For the Ancient Egyptians, the divine nature of the universe was manifested in a multitude of ways. Their gods, for example, could appear in the guise of animals, illustrating a fundamental belief that all forms of life were an expression of the divine. Similarly, the sky and its heavenly bodies, as well as a number of environmental and climatic features of Egypt, were embodied by deities such as Nut, who personified the sky, and Hapy, who was the god of the annual Nile inundation.

The manifestations of the gods

The gods of Ancient Egypt often had several aspects and could appear in different ways. Thoth, for example, was associated with the movement and power of the moon, although he was better known as a god of writing and knowledge, and could be depicted with the head of either an ibis or a baboon.

The process of syncretism, by which two or more deities were combined to form a single cult, was also central to religion in Ancient Egypt. Two of the most important deities, Amun and Ra, for example, were fused to create Amun-Ra. In the Ptolemaic Period (332–30 BC), Ptolemy I (305–285 BC) created Serapis, a combination of the Greek gods Zeus and Helios with Osiris and Apis, perhaps in a move towards political and cultural unity.

▲ **Depiction of hybrid deities**
The solar cult was one of the central features of Ancient Egyptian religion. The sun god, Ra, had numerous forms, including Ra-Horakhty, shown above, a combination of Ra and Horus.

INSIGHT

Osiris, god of the afterlife

Along with the sun god, Ra, Osiris, the primary god of the dead, was one of the most important deities in the pantheon. In Ancient Egyptian mythology, Osiris was killed by his evil brother Seth, and his dismembered body was mummified and resurrected by his wife Isis.

During the Old Kingdom (2686–2181 BC), the deceased pharaoh was identified with Osiris and was believed to experience rebirth in the same way that the murdered god did. During the First Intermediate period (2181–2055 BC), however, it seems that it became possible for commoners to be resurrected in the manner of Osiris, as a sort of 'democratization of the afterlife' took place. Mummification was designed to make the deceased resemble Osiris as much as possible, in the hope that this would ensure eternal life in the underworld.

Osiris presided over the weighing of the heart ceremony in the afterlife. In this ritual, the deceased made the 'negative confession', swearing that they had not committed any of a list of offences, then their heart was weighed against the feather of Maat, symbol of truth and harmony. Osiris judged the results of the ritual and was responsible for deciding whether the deceased was worthy of resurrection.

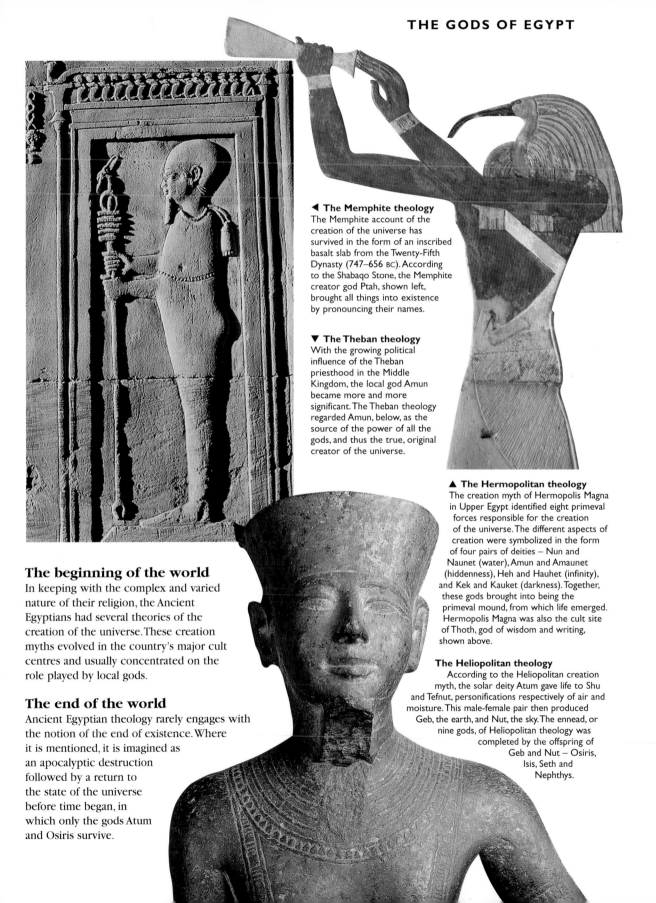

◄ The Memphite theology
The Memphite account of the creation of the universe has survived in the form of an inscribed basalt slab from the Twenty-Fifth Dynasty (747–656 BC). According to the Shabaqo Stone, the Memphite creator god Ptah, shown left, brought all things into existence by pronouncing their names.

▼ The Theban theology
With the growing political influence of the Theban priesthood in the Middle Kingdom, the local god Amun became more and more significant. The Theban theology regarded Amun, below, as the source of the power of all the gods, and thus the true, original creator of the universe.

▲ The Hermopolitan theology
The creation myth of Hermopolis Magna in Upper Egypt identified eight primeval forces responsible for the creation of the universe. The different aspects of creation were symbolized in the form of four pairs of deities – Nun and Naunet (water), Amun and Amaunet (hiddenness), Heh and Hauhet (infinity), and Kek and Kauket (darkness). Together, these gods brought into being the primeval mound, from which life emerged. Hermopolis Magna was also the cult site of Thoth, god of wisdom and writing, shown above.

The Heliopolitan theology
According to the Heliopolitan creation myth, the solar deity Atum gave life to Shu and Tefnut, personifications respectively of air and moisture. This male-female pair then produced Geb, the earth, and Nut, the sky. The ennead, or nine gods, of Heliopolitan theology was completed by the offspring of Geb and Nut – Osiris, Isis, Seth and Nephthys.

The beginning of the world

In keeping with the complex and varied nature of their religion, the Ancient Egyptians had several theories of the creation of the universe. These creation myths evolved in the country's major cult centres and usually concentrated on the role played by local gods.

The end of the world

Ancient Egyptian theology rarely engages with the notion of the end of existence. Where it is mentioned, it is imagined as an apocalyptic destruction followed by a return to the state of the universe before time began, in which only the gods Atum and Osiris survive.

Foreign Gods on the Nile

Egypt's overseas conquests, and the incursions of foreign rulers, brought its people into contact with many different deities; several were worshipped in Egypt, either in their own right or incorporated in an Egyptian god.

The letter of a New Kingdom priestess from Memphis to her counterpart in Thebes asks for a blessing from a long list of deities: 'Ptah who is south of his wall … Baalat, Kadesh, Anat, Baal, Zaphon … and all gods who are in Memphis.' Of these, only Ptah was Egyptian in origin. The text clearly illustrates how gods and goddesses from other countries in the region were apparently worshipped on the same level as the many native members of the pantheon. Although the cults of Baal and Anat had been deeply rooted in the Delta from the time of the Hyksos kings from Palestine (1650–1550 BC), the great majority of these foreign gods had been introduced to Egypt during the New Kingdom (1550–1069 BC), as the pharaohs established strong cultural and trade links with Egypt's neighbours.

A few cults were devoted to gods that originated in Nubia, Libya, or, like Sopdu, the lands east of Egypt, but the great majority of foreign gods in Egypt derived from Syria-Palestine, reflecting the many incursions of pharaohs there during the New Kingdom.

Gods from Phoenicia, Canaan and Syria, including Astarte, Kadesh and Reshef, were widely worshipped throughout Egypt by the end of the New Kingdom. Memphis, a military city with a harbour and the hub of many trade routes, had a particularly large foreign population. Temples and small sanctuaries for Baal, Reshef, Astarte and Kadesh were even built within the confines of the large temple devoted to Ptah.

Min, god of male potency, is the only one of the triad to have originated in Egypt.

◄ The gods of war
This small statue adopts a familiar Egyptian pose, stepping forwards with his left leg, and wears a headdress similar to the white crown of Upper Egypt, but is Phoenician in origin. The weapons the figurine once brandished are long gone, but he is identifiable as the warrior god Baal. As early as the Middle Kingdom, but particularly in the Ramesside period, the Egyptian god of chaos, storms and the weather, Seth, became known as 'lord of the foreign lands'. The 'marriage' of warlike Baal and the tempestuous Seth to form the bellicose Seth-Baal was perhaps inevitable.

Three lotus flowers in the right hand of the goddess Kadesh symbolize sexuality and fertility.

▲ A powerful trio
The Syrian goddess Kadesh is usually depicted naked (or in a transparent robe) and is shown front-on rather than in profile. She typically stands on the back of a lion, holding flowers in her right hand and snakes in her left. She was so far integrated into Egyptian religious beliefs that she formed part of a triad with another Syrian god, the warlike Reshef, and the ithyphallic Egyptian fertility god, Min.

Hathor's headdress and hair identify Kadesh as a goddess of sex and fertility.

The snake in her left hand signifies the power of Kadesh to ward off evil.

The Amorite war god Reshef is depicted wearing the white crown of Upper Egypt, but with a gazelle's head in place of the uraeus.

▶ A badge of fertility

This sistrum carries an image of Hathor, goddess of love, music and dance in Egypt from the earliest times. Hathor's distinctive curling wig, cow's ears or headdress of wig, horns and sun disc were applied to foreign goddesses introduced to Egypt as a sign of their powers over sex and fertility.

▼ Foreign worshippers, local gods

From the New Kingdom, foreigners who settled in the Nile Valley worshipped their own gods while propitiating native deities. Persians living in Memphis in the Twenty-Seventh Dynasty (525–404 BC) commissioned stelae on which they were shown wearing their own costumes, but carved in Egyptian style, making offerings in front of Egyptian gods.

A mixture of religions

The gods of Near Eastern origin worshipped in pharaonic Egypt generally kept their names. As they were frequently equated with the traditional Egyptian gods and deities, their depictions were often adapted to Egyptian beliefs: thus, their attributes could be the crowns, wigs and sceptres of Egyptian gods. Their cults concentrated on areas where large numbers of foreigners lived and worked. The goddess Kadesh, for example, was much revered in the workmen's settlement of Deir el-Medina.

Foreign gods in Egypt tended to keep their traits, history and human faces - animal-headed gods were rare outside Egypt. Thus Anat, a Syrian goddess, remains a mannish, bellicose figure equipped with a battle-axe and shield. Although they retained their original character, foreign gods were often identified with their Egyptian counterparts. Baal, god of storms, was assimilated in Seth, his equivalent in Egypt, while Kadesh, a Syrian generative goddess, was confounded with Hathor.

The gods of Olympus

After Alexander the Great conquered Egypt in 332 BC, the country's new rulers brought the Greek gods with them. The Ptolemies particularly venerated Dionysos, and held great festivals in Alexandria in his honour, but the local people continued to worship their old gods.

Ptolemy I Soter I (305-285 BC) tried to bring the two cultures together by creating a new god, Serapis, with traits of various Greek and Egyptian gods; his appearance was based on Zeus, the chief Greek god, who had no great cult in Egypt. The veneration of Serapis (the name derives from two Egyptian gods, Osiris and Apis) was centred on the Serapeum in Alexandria, a temple built on classical Greek lines; none of it survives today.

◀ **A new deity**
The Greek pharaoh Ptolemy I Soter I (305-285 BC) introduced a new god with Greek and Egyptian characteristics, to be worshipped in Alexandria. Depicted in Greek style, the bearded Serapis was essentially the Egyptian god Osorapis – himself a fusion of Osiris and Apis – with the attributes of various Greek deities, notably Zeus and Dionysos. Isis was made his consort.

◀◀ **King of the gods**
Zeus, the highest of the Greek gods, was incorporated in the syncretic deity Serapis in Egypt. The cult of Serapis was adopted by the Romans and spread through the empire; a head of Serapis was unearthed at the Walbrook Mithraeum in London.

Dionysos, assimilated in Osiris, supposedly founded the Amun oracle in the desert.

◀ **The melding of the gods**
Under the Ptolemies (305–30 BC), the Egyptian pantheon grew ever more crowded as the Greek kings attempted to promote the cultural assimilation of the Egyptian people by merging various gods from the Greek pantheon with native Egyptian deities. Dionysos, god of wine and ecstatic states, was identified, for example, with Osiris. Egyptian gods that did keep their traditional identity – such as Isis – were often depicted in Greek robes and carved in the more detailed, naturalistic style of Ancient Greece.

The cult of Isis, who kept her name under the Ptolemies, continued to be strong throughout the Roman period.

◀ **Hermes Trismegistos**
The Greeks equated Thoth, Egyptian god of wisdom and writing, with Hermes, messenger of the gods (Mercury in the Roman pantheon). The cult city of Thoth, Khmun, was renamed Hermopolis Magna, 'Great city of Hermes', and the Greeks applied the epithet Trismegistos ('thrice great') to Thoth as they did to Hermes. Under the Greeks and Romans, elements of the scientific and arcane wisdom and religious beliefs of the Ancient Egyptians were collected as *Corpus Hermeticum*, so called because Thoth was the scribe of the gods. The *Corpus* was the basis of the spiritual science of alchemy and several European magical systems in what is now known as the hermetic tradition. The secrecy of these writings has led to the use of the word 'hermetic' to mean 'sealed'.

▲ **The birth of Aphrodite**
This piece of decorative fabric from the Coptic Christian period shows the birth of the Greek goddess Aphrodite (the Roman Venus) on a wave. In the Ptolemaic period, she tended to be equated in Egypt with Hathor; Aphrodite was the goddess of love, and Hathor was the 'lady of grace, sweet in love'. Both were capable, too, of a punishing ruthlessness in their dealings with both gods and people who displeased them. The temple of Hathor at Dendera has a Greek inscription that shows the Greeks were fully aware of the correspondences between the two goddesses.

Popular belief

During the Greco-Roman epoch, as in preceding periods, many other gods were more popular with the commoners than those revered by official religion.

The great gods supported by the state presumably seemed too unapproachable to ordinary men and women to be bothered with their everyday needs and worries. Instead, people turned to 'smaller' gods such as Harpocrates, the son of Isis and Osiris. Because of his own fate, having to fend off the manifold dangers of poisonous animals, he seemed perfectly suitable to protect people as well. Numerous terracotta figures of the god are proof of his enormous popularity.

The Creation Myth of Hermopolis

The main cosmologies – theories explaining the creation of the universe – of Ancient Egypt were elaborated by priests in three great religious centres: Heliopolis, city of Ra; Memphis, city of Ptah; and Hermopolis Magna, city of Thoth and the Ogdoad.

The great Egyptian cult-centre of Khmun was renamed Hermopolis Magna in the Greco-Roman period (332 BC–AD 395), but the creation myth associated with it is truly ancient, with some of the gods and ideas mentioned in the *Pyramid Texts* of the Old Kingdom (2686–2181 BC). As with many Ancient Egyptian texts, the cosmology of Hermopolis has not survived as a single account, but has to be deduced from fragments and references in other texts, most of them from the New Kingdom (1550–1069 BC).

It begins, like the other Egyptian myths of the birth of the universe, with a dark world covered by Nun, a featureless ocean of unknown age, depth and extent, symbolizing chaos and the unformed. It is not difficult to see the origins of this image in the way the annual Nile flood covered the land, and, in the same way that the waters silently deposited fertilizing silt on the inundated fields, so the inchoate dark mass of Nun sheltered and nurtured the creative energies that would bring the world into being.

The Ogdoad

In the Hermopolis cosmology, this creative force was embodied by four gods and four goddesses, paired up to represent four qualities or principles within the primeval ocean. Known collectively as the Ogdoad, from the Greek word for a set of eight, they were Nun and Naunet, representing water; Kek and Kauket, darkness; Heh and Hauhet, infinity or formlessness; and Amun and Amaunet, air or latent power.

Egg-shaped models are not uncommon in Egyptian tombs. The spiral decoration represents the cracking of the shell as the sun emerges.

▼ Mythical origins

The annual flood of the Nile, when the rising waters covered its banks and deposited their load of silt before receding to reveal small hummocks of very fertile soil, inspired the Egyptian belief in the existence of a limitless mass of water that preceded creation. This began with the emergence of the first land, known as the primeval mound in other cosmologies and the 'island of flames' in Hermopolis.

▶ The primeval egg

In the creation myth of Hermopolis, the Ogdoad did not create the world themselves, but prepared the way by sending out from the ocean a creator god that had yet to emerge into consciousness. According to one version of the myth, the creative solar god emerged from a primeval egg. The Ancient Egyptian sources do not agree on how this egg came into being. One tradition has it that the egg was modelled by the gods and goddesses of the Ogdoad and fertilized by the breath of Amun. In another account, the egg was laid by a bird, which at Hermopolis was identified as the sacred ibis, an incarnation of Thoth. In all versions, though, the egg was placed on the dry land of the primeval mound, where it would hatch out the sun, the true creator of the universe.

◀ **The goddesses of the Ogdoad**
The four female gods of the Ogdoad were represented in the form of snakes, or as figures with serpent heads. As snakes were the first animals to reappear after the waters of the Nile floods had receded, they were naturally chosen as manifestations of the goddesses to partner the frog gods.

▼ **Lords of creation**
The choice of frogs to manifest the male gods of the Ogdoad reflects the Egyptians' keen observation of the natural world. The frog's aquatic habits and origins would have made it at home in the primeval ocean, while its extraordinary life cycle, in which it metamorphoses from tadpole to adult, represented both the transition from chaos to creation and the rebirth of the dead in the afterlife.

▲ **The divine couple**
One of the four pairs of deities in the Ogdoad, Amun and Amaunet, personified the entire male or female force of the Ogdoad. As Amun was raised by the priests of Thebes to be venerated as the main creator god, Amaunet lost her place as his chief wife to the goddess Mut. She is, however, honoured alongside Amun in the temple of Deir el-Hagar in the Dakhla Oasis in the Libyan desert, 300km (186 miles) west of the Nile.

PRIVATE TEMPLES – PUBLIC PAGEANTS

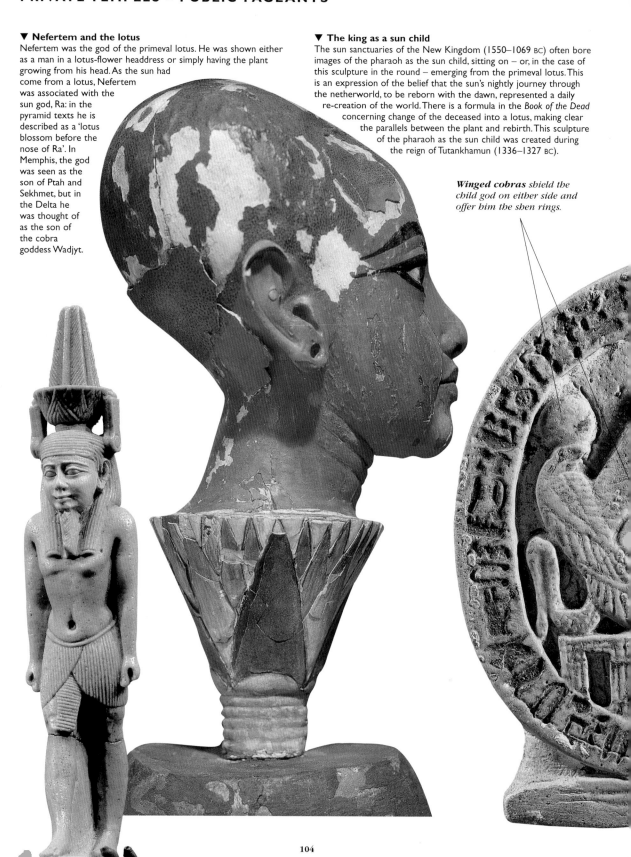

▼ Nefertem and the lotus

Nefertem was the god of the primeval lotus. He was shown either as a man in a lotus-flower headdress or simply having the plant growing from his head. As the sun had come from a lotus, Nefertem was associated with the sun god, Ra: in the pyramid texts he is described as a 'lotus blossom before the nose of Ra'. In Memphis, the god was seen as the son of Ptah and Sekhmet, but in the Delta he was thought of as the son of the cobra goddess Wadjyt.

▼ The king as a sun child

The sun sanctuaries of the New Kingdom (1550–1069 BC) often bore images of the pharaoh as the sun child, sitting on – or, in the case of this sculpture in the round – emerging from the primeval lotus. This is an expression of the belief that the sun's nightly journey through the netherworld, to be reborn with the dawn, represented a daily re-creation of the world. There is a formula in the *Book of the Dead* concerning change of the deceased into a lotus, making clear the parallels between the plant and rebirth. This sculpture of the pharaoh as the sun child was created during the reign of Tutankhamun (1336–1327 BC).

Winged cobras shield the child god on either side and offer him the shen rings.

▼ The amulet of Osorkon

The inscription around this amulet, depicting the creation myth of the primeval lotus, identifies its original owner as Prince Osorkon, whose ancestors became powerful as rulers of a Libyan tribe, the Ma, in the Third Intermediate period (1069–747 BC). A child with a finger placed to his lips sits on an open flower. In his right hand, he holds the heka, or crook, a sign of royal power, while the disc on his head signifies the newborn sun. Two protective cobras offer him a shen ring, symbol of eternity and infinity. The amulet itself is in the shape of a shen ring, making it a powerful charm promoting rebirth into a new life.

The youth curl, a sidelock conventionally used to denote princes in reliefs, helps identify the figure as the sun child.

The band of inscriptions around the amulet's rim lists the names and titles of Osorkon.

There are several versions of how the Ogdoad brought the world into being. One is that their collective will created the first dry land – the 'island of flames' or 'island of fire' – in the primeval ocean. There, the primeval gods created their 'son', an egg, which was fertilized by the breath of air – Amun – producing the god of creation. In Hermopolis, this god was probably equated to Thoth.

Emerging from chaos

Another version is that the Ogdoad propelled a lotus flower from the water; from this emerged the creator in the shape of a beetle (a manifestation of the rising sun), finally taking the shape of a child with his finger placed on his lips – the newly risen sun child.

With their work done, the members of the Ogdoad died and were buried on the west bank at Thebes, on the site of the temple of Medinet Habu. Their demise did not render the eight gods of the Ogdoad inert; from their tomb, they continued to watch over the Nile floods.

▼ Offering the lotus

Many of the abundant aquatic plants in the Nile wetlands have attracted rich religious symbolism, but few more so than the blue lotus, which has flowers that close in the evening and open at sunrise, making it a symbol of creation being renewed every day. The central position of the lotus in the Hermopolis creation myth was expressed in the ritual of 'offering a golden lotus', illustrated in this relief and performed by the city's priests on behalf of the pharaoh: 'Receive the golden lotus that gave birth to creation and chased away the darkness without anyone having witnessed it.'

Priests, Servants of the Gods

In theory, the pharaoh, as the the high priest of every cult, was the only person permitted to worship the gods. But even the king could not be in more than one sanctuary at the same time, and priests were required for the daily rituals in the temples.

Every city in Egypt honoured its own god, but the importance of the deity – and thus the clergy at its service – depended on the rank of the city. For a long time Amun was a minor god, worshipped in an obscure little town in Upper Egypt; however, when Thebes was promoted to capital, Amun moved up the hierarchy to become king of the gods. Originally, Amun was served by only a few head priests and a modest chapel, but, when he became god of the Egyptian empire, he had the largest clergy in Egypt.

The priestly hierarchy

The clergy in the great temples were organized in a strict hierarchy, although the details vary widely with place and period. At the summit was the chief priest, or 'first prophet', effectively the pharaoh's personal representative, and a few high-ranking priests who assisted him. As the only officials permitted to approach the god's statue enclosed in the sanctuary, these priests wielded considerable power, both religious and secular, controlling the wealth in the temple's treasury and the lands of its estates. They monitored both the 'lector' priests, who wrote the religious treatises and copied the

Water for purifying the food offerings to the temple's god was poured by wab priests from the inscribed bes-vase.

▼ **Dwelling place of the gods**
The temple was entrenched behind a plain brick wall that protected it from attack from the outside world – and from evil influences that could threaten the statue, the receptacle of the deity. The priests had to be pure and clean in order to work in the temple complex.

The terracotta basin collected the water that was poured during ceremonial purifications.

The golden cup was, like the bes-vase, a sacred artefact of temple ritual.

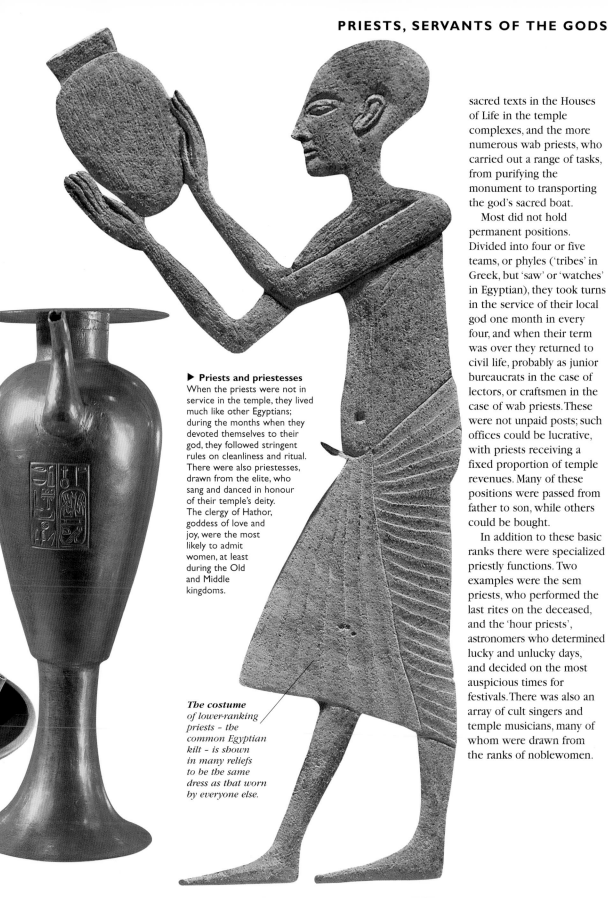

sacred texts in the Houses of Life in the temple complexes, and the more numerous wab priests, who carried out a range of tasks, from purifying the monument to transporting the god's sacred boat.

Most did not hold permanent positions. Divided into four or five teams, or phyles ('tribes' in Greek, but 'saw' or 'watches' in Egyptian), they took turns in the service of their local god one month in every four, and when their term was over they returned to civil life, probably as junior bureaucrats in the case of lectors, or craftsmen in the case of wab priests. These were not unpaid posts; such offices could be lucrative, with priests receiving a fixed proportion of temple revenues. Many of these positions were passed from father to son, while others could be bought.

In addition to these basic ranks there were specialized priestly functions. Two examples were the sem priests, who performed the last rites on the deceased, and the 'hour priests', astronomers who determined lucky and unlucky days, and decided on the most auspicious times for festivals. There was also an array of cult singers and temple musicians, many of whom were drawn from the ranks of noblewomen.

▶ **Priests and priestesses**
When the priests were not in service in the temple, they lived much like other Egyptians; during the months when they devoted themselves to their god, they followed stringent rules on cleanliness and ritual. There were also priestesses, drawn from the elite, who sang and danced in honour of their temple's deity. The clergy of Hathor, goddess of love and joy, were the most likely to admit women, at least during the Old and Middle kingdoms.

The costume of lower-ranking priests – the common Egyptian kilt – is shown in many reliefs to be the same dress as that worn by everyone else.

Osiris and the priest

This illustration, based on the relief in a tomb in the Valley of the Kings, dating from the time of Rameses III (1184–1153 BC),

Osiris is wearing the solar disc, with a protective uraeus, fitted to the blue crown.

Isis, Lady of the Heaven, reads the hieroglyph above her profile.

▼ **Religious inspector**
Iteti, a dignitary of the Fourth Dynasty (2613–2494 BC), was an inspector of priests in the pyramid of Khafra. During the Old Kingdom (2686–2181 BC), a considerable clergy, attached to the royal funerary complex, worshipped the dead king.

Ruler of the underworld, Osiris was the god worshipped by the dead.

The deceased were also watched over by Isis, the supportive wife of Osiris.

The sem priest purifies the offerings of food and flowers presented to the gods with libations from a bes-vase.

The funerary sem priest is wearing a leopard skin.

Under the leopard skin, the sem priest is dressed in his everyday folded linen clothing.

Offerings to the gods consisted of foodstuffs, flowers and lotus buds, the symbols of rebirth.

When staying within the enclosure of the sanctuary, the priests lived in small houses reserved especially for them. They obeyed very strict rules of physical purity, shaving their heads and bodies, washing four times a day, and wearing only fine linen. Wool and leather were banned, and sandals were made from papyrus. The priests ate light food and obeyed all the dietary taboos.

The priests took part in the ritual of daily worship, the basic ceremony celebrated in the temples. Each dawn the statue of the god of the temple was 'awakened' by a high-ranking priest who entered the sanctuary alone to feed, wash, perfume and dress the deity. Outside the inner temple, priests brought offerings, sang hymns and purified the premises. Thus, the satisfied god would continue to help the pharaoh to maintain world order.

INSIGHT

Carrying the sacred boat

As depicted on the temple walls, most priests fulfilled only subordinate functions, one of which was to bear the model celestial barques that held the god's statue in procession, the shafts resting on their shoulders. This relief from the pillared court of the temple of Amun at Karnak shows priests wearing masks bearing the effigy of the genies of Lower Egypt with the head of a dog. The procession would stop for local people to pray to the god, or to call on the deity to pronounce oracles.

Karnak was the venue for the greatest of Egypt's annual processions, part of the feast of Opet, when a team of priests carried ceremonial boats through throngs of revellers to the River Nile for their journey to Luxor and back.

◀ **Death in the face of the gods**
The pharaoh was the only person allowed to make offerings to the gods in the temples, and is therefore the only one depicted in the presence of the gods on temple walls. However, in the tombs – dedicated to the worship of the dead, rather than the gods – the deceased had the opportunity to earn favours from the deities by making offerings. In this nineteenth-century drawing by Prisse d'Avennes, Osiris is receiving both an offering and a libation from a sem priest.

◀ **Sacred waters**
The sacred lake of the huge temple complex of Amun at Karnak, near Luxor, was bordered on one side by the priests' houses. Every day after dawn, before entering the monument, the officiating priests climbed down the steps of the rectangular, stone-lined reservoir to purify themselves in the holy water.

The Statue of Ka-aper

One of the masterpieces of Old Kingdom private sculpture, the life-size standing figure of chief lector priest Ka-aper is remarkable for its astonishing realism, and is among the most frequently viewed objects in the Egyptian Museum in Cairo.

This statue was discovered by Auguste Mariette during excavations in Saqqara in 1860. Local workmen named it 'Sheikh el-Beled', Arabic for 'headman of the village', because of its subject's striking similarity to the chief of their village.

The figure, which bears no inscription, is carved from the wood of the sycomore fig tree, which had a strong symbolic meaning in Egypt: the sycomore was associated with the goddess Hathor and the netherworld.

The sculpture was found in the mastaba tomb of the chief lector priest Ka-aper. Next to it were two further wooden statues – one of Ka-aper's wife, the other of the priest as a young man.

Remarkable realism

The body and head of the figure are made from a single piece of wood, to which the arms, carved separately, were attached. The pose is unusual in Egyptian statuary, in that the legs show a walking movement rather than a rigid stance. This, along with the priest's expressive face and striking eyes, makes the statue remarkably lifelike.

The original cane and sceptre held in his hands were missing, and the cane the priest now holds is a modern reproduction. The legs have also been partly restored. Ka-aper's plump, rounded body is wrapped in a knee-length loincloth, knotted at the waist with a large flap.

The statue is one of the most highly regarded works of the Old Kingdom and perfectly captures the physical and psychological characteristics of the dignified, wealthy man that Ka-aper was.

▶ **Ka-aper, a lector priest of the Old Kingdom**
Measuring 112cm (44 inches) in height, this statue, now in the Egyptian Museum, Cairo, is one of the finest works of art from the Old Kingdom (2686–2181 BC). It is an image of a high-ranking official and chief lector priest – he recited the words of the gods in temple rituals – of the late Fourth or early Fifth Dynasty. It was found in his tomb in north Saqqara near the pyramid complex of the Fifth Dynasty pharaoh Userkaf (2494–2487 BC).

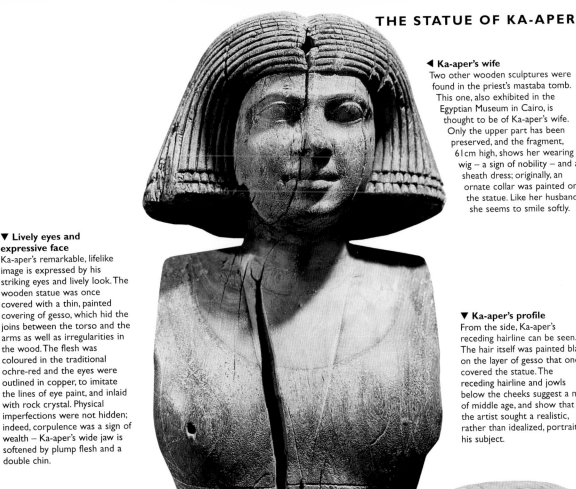

◀ Ka-aper's wife
Two other wooden sculptures were found in the priest's mastaba tomb. This one, also exhibited in the Egyptian Museum in Cairo, is thought to be of Ka-aper's wife. Only the upper part has been preserved, and the fragment, 61cm high, shows her wearing a wig – a sign of nobility – and a sheath dress; originally, an ornate collar was painted onto the statue. Like her husband, she seems to smile softly.

▼ Lively eyes and expressive face
Ka-aper's remarkable, lifelike image is expressed by his striking eyes and lively look. The wooden statue was once covered with a thin, painted covering of gesso, which hid the joins between the torso and the arms as well as irregularities in the wood. The flesh was coloured in the traditional ochre-red and the eyes were outlined in copper, to imitate the lines of eye paint, and inlaid with rock crystal. Physical imperfections were not hidden; indeed, corpulence was a sign of wealth – Ka-aper's wide jaw is softened by plump flesh and a double chin.

▼ Ka-aper's profile
From the side, Ka-aper's receding hairline can be seen. The hair itself was painted black on the layer of gesso that once covered the statue. The receding hairline and jowls below the cheeks suggest a man of middle age, and show that the artist sought a realistic, rather than idealized, portrait of his subject.

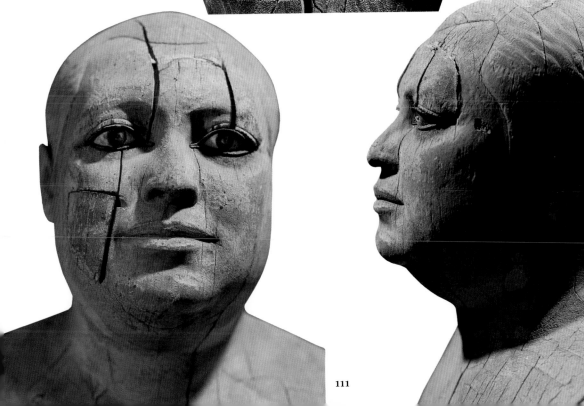

The Sed Festival

To regenerate his strength and renew his power, the pharaoh celebrated by holding a festival known in Egyptian as the heb sed *(royal jubilee). In principle, this complex ceremony took place in the thirtieth year of his reign and, thereafter, every two or three years.*

Although, in theory, the king could celebrate his jubilee only after a reign of 30 years, in practice, rulers such as Hatshepsut (1473–1458 BC) held it earlier to reaffirm their power. Not all pharaohs had sed festivals; the first recorded one was conducted by Den of the First Dynasty (3100–2686 BC), and the earliest surviving architectural evidence of the ceremony is the sed festival courtyard in the funerary complex of the step pyramid of Djoser (2667–2648 BC) at Saqqara.

The elaborate rituals varied from sed to sed, with some rulers taking a low-key approach, while others, such as Hatshepsut, Amenhotep III (1390–1352 BC) and Rameses II (1279–1213 BC), enjoyed lavish ceremonies that lasted for days.

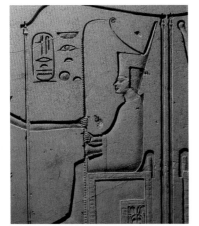

◀ **The costume of the sed festival**
On this relief from the temple of Montu, god of war, at Medamud, Senusret III (1874–1855 BC) is dressed for his sed festival. He wears a long white garment from which only his head and his hands – holding the notched palm branch symbol of longevity – emerge. On his head is the red crown, and to his back a mirror image (not pictured) shows him wearing the white crown. The symbol of the union of the two Egypts is depicted on the side of the throne.

▼ **The courtyard and chapels of the sed festival**
The jubilee was not only for the living king, but also for the deceased. Following his death, the ruler (it was believed) continued to celebrate his sed in the afterlife. In his funerary complex at Saqqara, dominated by the step pyramid, Djoser (2683–2643 BC) built the courtyard and chapels for just such a purpose.

The flail in Queen Hatshepsut's right hand is a symbol of royal authority.

The straight false beard is worn by ruling pharaohs.

The apis bull, the sacred animal of the god Ptah of Memphis, accompanies the ruler during the ritual run.

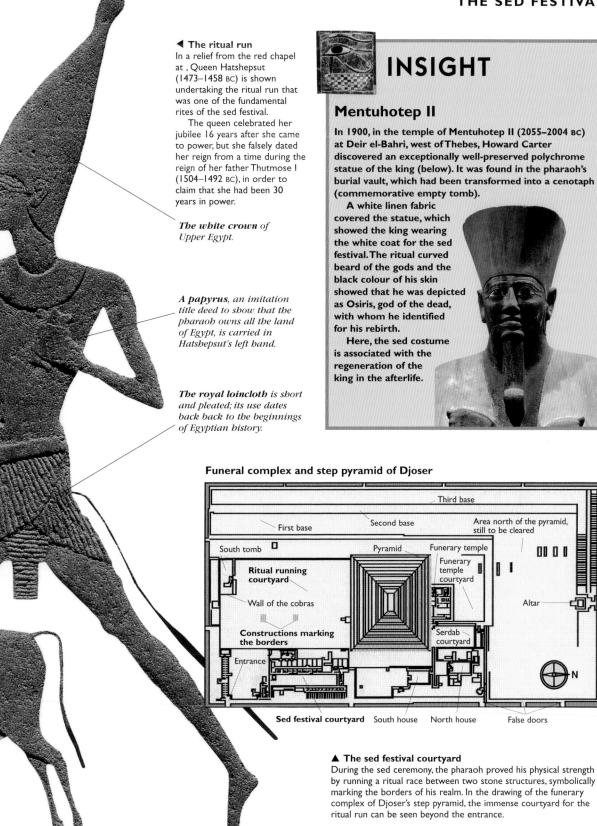

◀ **The ritual run**
In a relief from the red chapel at , Queen Hatshepsut (1473–1458 BC) is shown undertaking the ritual run that was one of the fundamental rites of the sed festival.

The queen celebrated her jubilee 16 years after she came to power, but she falsely dated her reign from a time during the reign of her father Thutmose I (1504–1492 BC), in order to claim that she had been 30 years in power.

The white crown of Upper Egypt.

A papyrus, an imitation title deed to show that the pharaoh owns all the land of Egypt, is carried in Hatshepsut's left hand.

The royal loincloth is short and pleated; its use dates back back to the beginnings of Egyptian history.

INSIGHT

Mentuhotep II

In 1900, in the temple of Mentuhotep II (2055–2004 BC) at Deir el-Bahri, west of Thebes, Howard Carter discovered an exceptionally well-preserved polychrome statue of the king (below). It was found in the pharaoh's burial vault, which had been transformed into a cenotaph (commemorative empty tomb).

A white linen fabric covered the statue, which showed the king wearing the white coat for the sed festival. The ritual curved beard of the gods and the black colour of his skin showed that he was depicted as Osiris, god of the dead, with whom he identified for his rebirth.

Here, the sed costume is associated with the regeneration of the king in the afterlife.

Funeral complex and step pyramid of Djoser

Third base

First base Second base Area north of the pyramid, still to be cleared

South tomb Pyramid Funerary temple

Ritual running courtyard Funerary temple courtyard

Wall of the cobras Altar

Constructions marking the borders

Serdab courtyard

Entrance

N

Sed festival courtyard South house North house False doors

▲ **The sed festival courtyard**
During the sed ceremony, the pharaoh proved his physical strength by running a ritual race between two stone structures, symbolically marking the borders of his realm. In the drawing of the funerary complex of Djoser's step pyramid, the immense courtyard for the ritual run can be seen beyond the entrance.

Monumental halls and courtyards were often built to hold the royal jubilee, which began on the morning that the Nile flood began to subside. Surrounded by the royal court and senior dignitaries, the pharaoh would first raise the djed pillar, representing the backbone of Osiris, god of resurrection, and symbolizing stability.

Next, the king re-enacted his coronation, successively mounting two thrones wearing the crowns of Upper and Lower Egypt to reaffirm his authority over all of Egypt. Later in the day, the king undertook a ritual run, often in a specially prepared courtyard, between two sets of boundary markers representing the borders of his domain. Once the ceremonial rites were over, there were days of singing, dancing and feasting on beer, bread and beef, as well as the exchange of gifts and souvenirs.

Varying the rituals

Although there were certain rites central to sed festivals, it appears that the symbolism and events were sometimes adapted to suit the times and the occasion. The introduction of the symbolic travelling by royal barge, to mimic the daily journey of the sun god, appeared during the New Kingdom (1550–1069 BC), and Amenhotep III even had a lake excavated for the journey.

▼ Hatshepsut's solar journey
This relief from the Red Chapel at Karnak shows the royal barge being carried to imitate the day and night travels of the sun god across the sky and through the underworld.

◄ The sed of an unknown king
This carved ivory standing figurine of an unknown king of the First Dynasty (3100–2890 BC) was discovered in a temple at Abydos. He is clothed in a garment usually worn at a sed festival. The detail of the quilted pattern of the fabric has been exceptionally well executed.

Two journeys were enacted in the royal barge – one for night-time; one for daytime – before the pharaoh was returned to the throne.

▶ Amenhotep III

In the thirtieth year of his reign, Amenhotep III (1390–1352 BC) celebrated the first of his three sed festivals. He built a special hall at Malkata on the west bank of the Nile at Thebes. Preparations for his festival were made years in advance, and Amenhotep III sent scribes to study temple archives and visit the ancient sites to re-create the sed ceremonies of his predecessors.

Hieroglyphs translate as 'Amun-Ra, giver of life and lord of the sky'.

Rising suns symbolize the daily cycle of death and rebirth of the sun and, as such, the regeneration of the pharaoh during the sed.

▼ Singing and dancing

This limestone relief comes from the tomb of Kheruef, steward of Queen Tiys (1410–1340 BC), and principal organizer of Amenhotep III's sed festival. The relief shows two unnamed royal children shaking sistra – special rattles used in the worship of Hathor, goddess of regeneration. She was said to suckle all pharaohs seeking rebirth and renewal of their physical and political power.

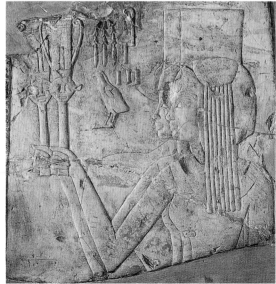

Participants in the festival were drawn from the royal court and high officials, and sometimes included specially invited foreign dignitaries.

The royal barge carried the pharaoh on the symbolic journey. In some sed festivals, this ceremony took place on a sacred lake.

The Opet Festival

On important dates, images of the gods were carried through the streets in a procession. One of these events was the Opet Festival, celebrated each year in honour of Amun.

In the temples of Ancient Egypt, only the first courtyard was accessible to the public. Entry to the inner area, or particularly the inner sanctuary where the cult image was kept, was reserved for the priests and the pharaoh. The common people could approach the cult statue itself only during rare and important festivals - but even then it was hidden from view in a shrine.

The journey of the gods

One such occasion was the Opet Festival, celebrated annually in the second month of the season of akhet, the inundation period. Initially, in the Eighteenth Dynasty (1550–1295 BC), it lasted 11 days, but, by the Twentieth Dynasty (1186–1069 BC), it continued for 27 days.

For this festival, the statues of Amun, Mut and Khons were taken from the Karnak temple to the temple at Luxor. In the beginning, the shrines with the cult images were carried overland from Karnak to Luxor on model divine barges; the return journey was made on the Nile. Later, the entire journey took place on the river, in a series of ceremonial boats.

▶ **The god Amun**
The Opet Festival was celebrated at Thebes in honour of Amun. The procession of the divine barges of Amun, his wife Mut and their son Khons from Karnak to Luxor took place with pomp and circumstance. It was the highlight of the festival, during which Amun renewed the pharaoh's right to power, ruling as a god on earth.

▼ **Overland procession**
The divine images were taken on their barges in a festive procession from Karnak to Luxor, as shown in this relief on the walls of the colonnade at Luxor, which was built by Amenhotep III (1390–1352 BC) and decorated by Tutankhamun (1336–1327 BC)

The offerings *dedicated to Amun are laid out on offerings tables along the processional route.*

Way stations*, placed at intervals along the sphinx-lined route, allowed the barge to be rested temporarily.*

Several priests *carried the divine barge and its shrine.*

▼ **Amun's travels**

The priests carried the sacred cult barge of Amun on their shoulders to the river, where it was placed on a large Nile boat to continue its journey. Originally, Amun travelled on the river only on the way back from the Luxor temple to Karnak, but later, the entire journey took place on the water. The Nile boat was towed by the royal barge, or pulled along by ropes from the bank.

INSIGHT

Modern festivals

Some Ancient Egyptian customs and festivals have survived into modern times. At Luxor, once a year, a festival in honour of Sheik Abu'l-Haggâg is celebrated, with the barge procession reflecting the Opet Festival. The high point is the anniversary of the historic arrival of the Sheik at the thirteenth-century mosque of Abu'l-Haggâg (below) at Luxor. There is a boat procession on the Nile, with a felucca mooring at the Luxor temple, just like Amun's barge.

The image of Amun is hidden from view in a protective shrine.

The stern and bow are decorated with a ram's head, the personification of Amun.

The pharaoh walks in front of the barge bearing the divine image.

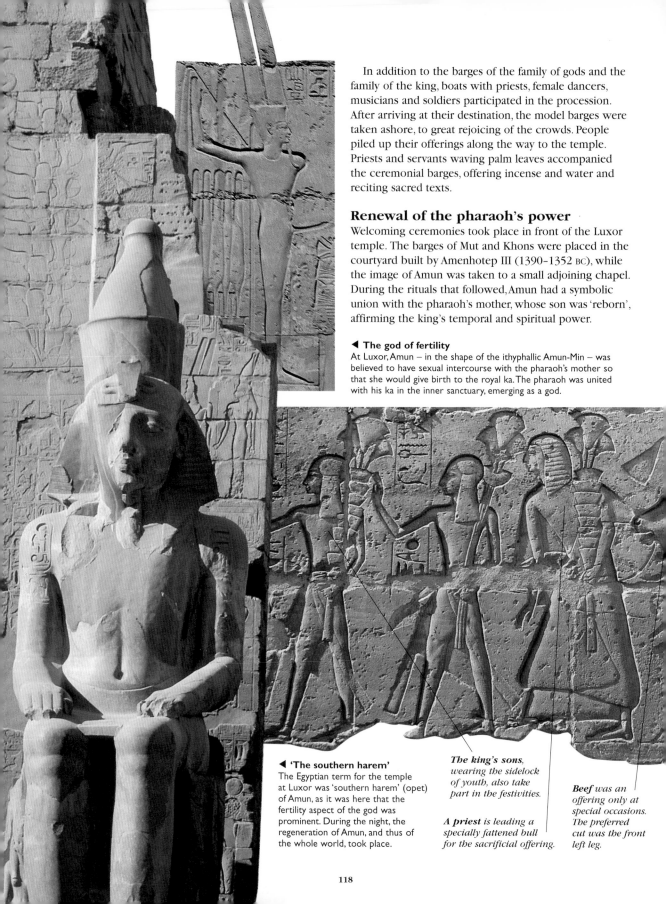

In addition to the barges of the family of gods and the family of the king, boats with priests, female dancers, musicians and soldiers participated in the procession. After arriving at their destination, the model barges were taken ashore, to great rejoicing of the crowds. People piled up their offerings along the way to the temple. Priests and servants waving palm leaves accompanied the ceremonial barges, offering incense and water and reciting sacred texts.

Renewal of the pharaoh's power

Welcoming ceremonies took place in front of the Luxor temple. The barges of Mut and Khons were placed in the courtyard built by Amenhotep III (1390–1352 BC), while the image of Amun was taken to a small adjoining chapel. During the rituals that followed, Amun had a symbolic union with the pharaoh's mother, whose son was 'reborn', affirming the king's temporal and spiritual power.

◀ **The god of fertility**
At Luxor, Amun – in the shape of the ithyphallic Amun-Min – was believed to have sexual intercourse with the pharaoh's mother so that she would give birth to the royal ka. The pharaoh was united with his ka in the inner sanctuary, emerging as a god.

◀ **'The southern harem'**
The Egyptian term for the temple at Luxor was 'southern harem' (opet) of Amun, as it was here that the fertility aspect of the god was prominent. During the night, the regeneration of Amun, and thus of the whole world, took place.

The king's sons, wearing the sidelock of youth, also take part in the festivities.

A priest is leading a specially fattened bull for the sacrificial offering.

Beef was an offering only at special occasions. The preferred cut was the front left leg.

▼ Musicians
Musicians, here playing lutes, formed part of the entourage that escorted the divine barges from the temple at Luxor during the Opet Festival.

▲ Libyans
Recognizable by their feathered headdresses, these Libyans are among the musicians in the procession. They are striking two clappers together, adding rhythm to the proceedings.

Offerings of conical loaves are carried by the priests who walk alongside the sacred bull.

▲ The offerings
During the Opet Festival, numerous cult rituals were performed, with a large number of small altars lining the streets. The king's offering took place at the temple.

119

The Funeral Cortège

Egyptian funerals were ceremonial occasions, which allowed the living to mourn the dead, and helped the deceased on his journey to the afterlife. Funeral processions were frequently depicted on the walls of tombs, particularly during the New Kingdom (1550–1069 BC).

For the life-loving Egyptians, the guarantee of continuing life in the netherworld was immensely important. After a person of high rank died, his corpse was mummified – a process that lasted 70 days; after this, his funeral could take place. The mummy was usually placed on a canopied, open-sided shrine. This was mounted on a boat-shaped bier which sat on a sled drawn by oxen.

Ritual mourning

Servants, priests and relatives all accompanied the funeral cortège. Of particular importance, however, were the professional mourners – wailing women who shouted lamentations, while beating their breasts and striking their heads on the ground (a tradition which persists to this day in North Africa). Various funerary goods and food offerings were also carried in the procession, destined for burial with the body.

▼ **The coffin enshrined**
This scene from the burial chamber of Tutankhamun's tomb shows the king's coffin resting in a canopied shrine decorated with sacred cobras. This is mounted on a boat-shaped bier, which in turn sits on a sled, drawn at the front of the cortège by oxen.

The goddess Nephthys stands on one side of the coffin to protect the deceased pharaoh.

DOCUMENT

Professional mourners

Wailing women – who were paid for their services – were an important presence at every Ancient Egyptian funeral. Usually dressed in pale blue, they let down their hair and tore at it, bared and beat their breasts, wept and wailed loudly, and struck their heads on the ground in a gesture of sorrow. The women's ritualized hysterical behaviour is depicted on this relief (below) from the tomb of Horemheb (1323–1295 BC) at Saqqara. Men displayed their grief in less ostentatious ways: they abstained from cutting their hair or beard for a certain period of time.

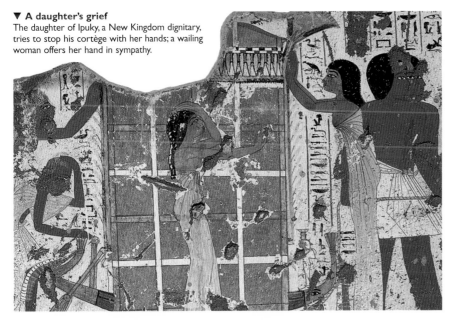

▼ A daughter's grief
The daughter of Ipuky, a New Kingdom dignitary, tries to stop his cortège with her hands; a wailing woman offers her hand in sympathy.

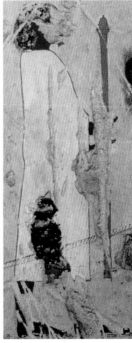

▲ Leading the cortège
At the funerals of kings and high officials, eminent dignitaries such as the vizier, here recognizable by his staff of office and distinctive cloak, walked in front of the sled carrying the coffin.

The hieroglyphs identify Tutankhamun with the god Osiris so that, like Osiris, the deceased king will be reborn in the afterlife.

Noblemen and courtiers wear ritual white bandages and white sandals as a sign of mourning.

The mourners use a rope to help pull the sled drawn in the front by oxen.

The two viziers of Upper and Lower Egypt (with bald heads) are among the courtiers who pull the shrine.

Wepwawet, the jackal god whose name means 'opener of the ways' and who protected the deceased on the route into the underworld, is shown on the standard at the prow of the boat-shaped bier.

The funeral cortège often made its way to the edge of the Nile. From there, it was taken by boat to the river's west bank, a voyage that symbolized the deceased's journey from the world of the living – the east bank of the Nile – to the world of the dead – the west bank.

The opening of the mouth ceremony

At the necropolis on the west bank, a tomb was prepared in advance to receive the mummy. Before the body was interred, however, certain rituals were performed. The most important of these was the 'opening of the mouth' ceremony, an elaborate procedure involving incantations and the purification and anointing of the mummified body that restored the dead person's faculties so that he or she could be reborn in the afterlife.

The final separation

Finally, the mummy was placed inside its coffin, which was taken down the vault into a burial chamber. Canopic jars and food supplies for the deceased, along with funerary furniture, were also deposited in the chamber before the tomb was sealed by local masons.

After the burial, family and guests enjoyed a feast of all kinds of food, wine and beer in honour of the dead. This took place outside the tomb, often in a special tent.

▶ **Tomb furnishings of Ramose, a New Kingdom vizier**
This scene comes from the tomb of Ramose, governor of Thebes and vizier in the time of Akhenaten (1352–1336 BC). In the afterlife, the deceased hoped to live in the same – or even better – style as he did when he was alive. For this reason, everything he needed in his former life was included in his tomb furnishings.

The several jars were probably filled with oil, wine and unguents.

A servant carries a chest and the leopard-skin garment worn in religious rituals.

◀ **Offerings to the spirit of the deceased**
In this scene from the tomb of vizier Ramose, the wailing women are preceded by four women in red and yellow robes with wigs of the same colour. Two present an offering of ritual bowls to the deceased.

INSIGHT

The journey across the Nile

To reach the necropolis on the west bank of the Nile, the funeral cortège had to cross the river by boat. The crossing symbolized the journey from the world of the living to the world of the dead, which was in the 'beautiful west', the location of the underworld.

The boat carrying the deceased was identified with neshmet, the barge of Osiris, the god with whom the deceased was likewise identified. In crossing the Nile, the deceased made a symbolic pilgrimage to Abydos, the site of Osiris's tomb.

This scene from the Eigtheenth-Dynasty tomb of Neferhotep in Thebes (below) depicts a funeral cortège crossing the Nile, accompanied by mourners, officials and relatives. A detail of a similar barge carrying the bier, along with rowers, can be seen at the bottom of the page.

The fan of ostrich plumes was attached to a wooden or metal handle.

An upholstered bed, complete with a black headrest (above the foot) was an indispensable item.

▼ **Middle Kingdom mourners**
The professional mourners of the Middle Kingdom (2055–1650 BC) can be distinguished from their New Kingdom counterparts by their tunic-

Treasures of the Afterlife

In ancient Egypt, power, influence and social status continued into the Afterlife. Hierarchies were often defined by the size of a tomb and the wealth it contained. But such treasures were also created in homage and appeasement to the gods. It was vital for Egyptians to know that they would be accepted into the next world, and they went to great lengths to ensure that the artefacts buried with them were appropriate for smoothing the way. So for instance, flasks containing organs of the deceased had to be the right flasks, decorated in the right way and with their contents deposited in the correct manner by priests and priestesses.

Such attention to detail meant that artisans were creating treasures as much for the deceased as for the living. The fine geometric patterns on their wares and the bucolic scenes of sacred rams and bulls were meant only for the eyes of the gods.

Today, grave goods give us a great insight into the everyday material culture of the Ancient Egyptians. However, most of the 'everyday objects' found in the tombs belonged not to the masses but to royalty and the upper classes. So when we see examples of tables and wood-framed chairs; elaborately decorated vases, mirrors and perfume flasks, it is as well to bear in mind that millions of artisans, labourers and street traders made do with basic pottery and stone urns, and rough-hewn wooden tables and seats sunk into thick sun-baked brick wall recesses.

Life after Death
Canopic jars such as these, dating from around 700 BC, were used to preserve the internal organs. Each jar is in the form of one of the sons of Horus: the jackal-headed Duamutef contained the stomach, the falcon-headed Qebhsenuef the intestines, and the human-headed Imsety the liver.

Life After Death

The Ancient Egyptians saw death not as the end, but as the beginning of a new existence. On their journey to the afterlife, they were accompanied by the material possessions they had used in this life, as well as food and drink to sustain them along the way.

The Ancient Egyptians believed that death was simply an interruption, rather than the end of life, and that the afterlife should consist of the best that was available and pleasurable in earthly existence. This could be brought about by various means. These included piety to the gods and the preservation of the body through mummification, along with the nourishment and protection of the spirit forms which survived death. At its most basic level, enjoyment of the afterlife could be achieved by burying the body with a set of funerary equipment, and at its most elaborate by building the painted and highly decorated tombs of royalty, complete with food, drink, tomb servants and other desirable objects.

The first step was the preservation of the body. As anatomical knowledge grew, embalmers were also able to preserve the internal organs. The body was dried out in natron, a compound of soda bicarbonate found naturally

Anubis and mummification

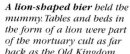

The jackal-headed god Anubis, watcher of the graveyards and conductor of souls, was the god of mummification. According to myth, he was able to restore life to the body of the murdered Osiris, the god of the dead and the ruler of the underworld, by embalming his corpse and wrapping it in linen.

The head and shoulders of the mummy were covered with a mummy mask, portraying an idealized image of the deceased.

A lion-shaped bier held the mummy. Tables and beds in the form of a lion were part of the mortuary cult as far back as the Old Kingdom.

INSIGHT

Canopic jars: vessels for internal organs

Organs taken from the body were completely dried, then anointed with sweet-smelling ointments, before being wrapped in linen, like the rest of the body, and stored in special vessels called Canopic jars. The name of these jars derived from the town of Canopus, in the Egyptian Delta, where a deity was worshipped in the form of a human-headed jar. The contents of the jar were placed under the protection of four minor gods called the Sons of Horus. The Canopic jars were stored in their own chest, which was drawn on a sled behind the sarcophagus in the funeral procession.

The human-headed Imsety looked after the liver.

The jackal-headed Duamutef guarded the stomach.

The ape-headed Hapy protected the lungs.

The falcon-headed Qebehsenuef looked after the intestines.

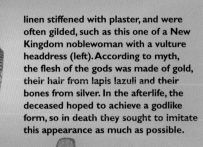

PROFILE

Mummy masks

As the dead had to be recognized in the afterlife, the linen-wrapped corpse was fitted with a mummy mask showing the idealized features of the deceased. Usually the masks were made of cartonnage, a material consisting of linen stiffened with plaster, and were often gilded, such as this one of a New Kingdom noblewoman with a vulture headdress (left). According to myth, the flesh of the gods was made of gold, their hair from lapis lazuli and their bones from silver. In the afterlife, the deceased hoped to achieve a godlike form, so in death they sought to imitate this appearance as much as possible.

Embalming priests assumed the identity of Anubis and in certain procedures wore a jackal mask. This was because everybody sought identification with Osiris at death, to ensure resurrection.

Linen bandages were used to wrap the mummified corpse after it had been coated with resin to toughen it and make it waterproof. As much as 375m² (4,040 sq ft) of linen were sometimes used.

◀ Decorated tombs

Much of our knowledge of Ancient Egyptian funerary practices comes from colourful wall paintings such as this one, showing the Anubis priest laying the last hand on the deceased.

It was found in the tomb of Sennedjem, a nobleman who lived during the Nineteenth Dynasty (c. 1200 BC), at Deir el Medina in western Thebes. Domestic scenes of Sennedjem and his wife also decorate the tomb.

▲ The heart scarab

Priests placed various protective amulets and charms between the many wrappings of linen. The wedjat eye, or eye of Horus (the symbol denoting the *Insight* box opposite), protected the body from any harm.

Of greater importance, however, was the heart scarab, placed over the heart. It was inscribed with extracts from the *Book of the Dead* (a collection of spells to counteract perils in the hereafter), urging the heart, as the seat of the soul, not to turn against its owner when his or her deeds and life were questioned by the gods during their trial and judgement.

in Egypt, then treated with salves and resins before being wrapped in linen bindings, sometimes as much as hundreds of metres long.

After the prepared mummy was placed in a sarcophagus, and the organs sealed in the Canopic jars, the funeral procession to the tomb began. The heaviest pieces, such as the sarcophagus and the jars, were hauled to the grave on sleds. The relatives and friends, and a long line of bearers, were accompanied by wailing and moaning women – professional mourners. Everything that the deceased needed in the afterlife was taken: chests of clothes and jewellery, furniture, perfumes and food, and sometimes – to show the scholarship of the deceased – writing materials. All of this, along with the sarcophagus and Canopic jars, was sealed in the chamber of the tomb.

The judgement of the dead

Before he entered the underworld, the deceased had first to face the divine tribunal. His earthly deeds were judged by 42 gods overseen by Osiris and many judgement scenes depict the weighing of the heart ceremony. In this ritual, the heart, representing a person's past deeds, was weighed against a feather, symbol of the justice of the gods. This test was only passed when the balance was level or in the heart's favour – and only then could the deceased travel on to eternity and the afterlife.

Funeral procession and burial offerings

Servants carrying grave goods formed a large part of the funeral procession. They transported everything the deceased might need in the afterlife – from furniture, jewellery and knicknacks to food, drink and perfumed oils – all to be buried alongside the body.

INSIGHT

Shabti figures

Also known as ushabtis, meaning 'answerers', these statuettes representing servants were placed in the burial chamber to carry out any menial work for the deceased in the hereafter. They have been found in large numbers and were made in a variety of materials, including pottery, wood and stone. Usually, they appear in the form of a mummy and are inscribed with the text from the *Book of the Dead* in which the shabti is commanded to carry out all necessary agricultural work for his master, including irrigating the fields. This typical example (right) is from the New Kingdom tomb of Mutemwija, the wife of Thutmosis IV (1397–1388 BC). Sometimes, tools such as hoes and picks, as well as baskets for grain, appear with the figures. Ideally, a tomb contained one figure for each day of the year, but some royal tombs contained many more.

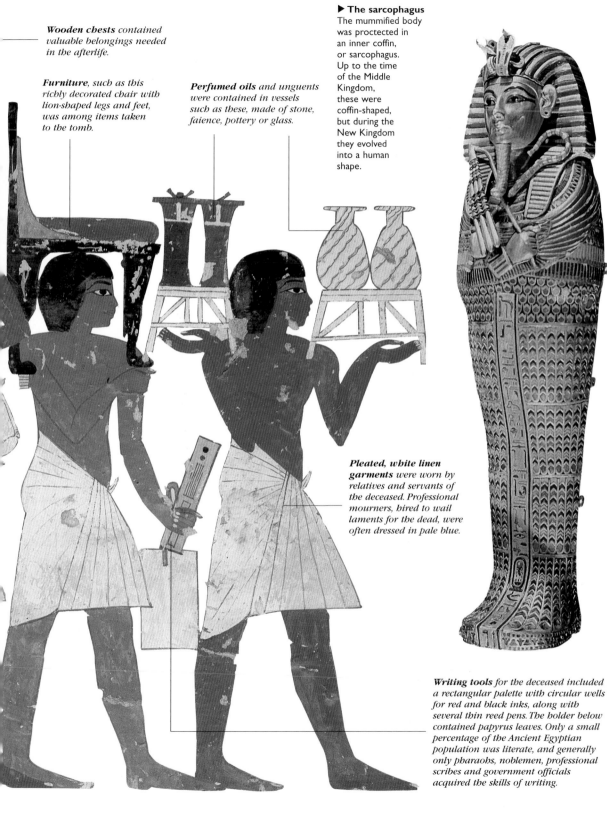

Wooden chests contained valuable belongings needed in the afterlife.

Furniture, such as this richly decorated chair with lion-shaped legs and feet, was among items taken to the tomb.

Perfumed oils and unguents were contained in vessels such as these, made of stone, faience, pottery or glass.

▶ **The sarcophagus**
The mummified body was proctected in an inner coffin, or sarcophagus. Up to the time of the Middle Kingdom, these were coffin-shaped, but during the New Kingdom they evolved into a human shape.

Pleated, white linen garments were worn by relatives and servants of the deceased. Professional mourners, hired to wail laments for the dead, were often dressed in pale blue.

Writing tools for the deceased included a rectangular palette with circular wells for red and black inks, along with several thin reed pens. The holder below contained papyrus leaves. Only a small percentage of the Ancient Egyptian population was literate, and generally only pharaohs, noblemen, professional scribes and government officials acquired the skills of writing.

The Ka, the Ba and the Akh

For the Egyptians, a person was made up of five parts which included two physical characteristics (his name and shadow) and three invisible elements – the ka (life force), the ba (similar to personality) and the akh (spirit).

The ka came into existence at the precise moment a human was born and continued as the individual's 'double' throughout life and after death. The creator god Khnum, for example, was often depicted modelling both the physical body and the ka on his potter's wheel. After death, the ka continued to live on and, like the deceased when he was alive, required food and drink. Food offerings, or depictions of them on tomb walls, sustained the ka, although he did not physically eat them, but absorbed their life-giving forces. Funerary statues were images of the deceased's ka, and sometimes wore the ka sign of a pair of raised arms as a headdress.

The ba was similar to the personality that makes an individual unique. However, it also represented power and could be extended to the gods and inanimate objects as well. Consequently, the ba was the physical form of certain gods: the Apis bull, for example, was the ba of Osiris. For the body of the deceased to survive in the afterlife, it had to be reunited with its ka every night. As the physical body was unable to do this, it was the duty of the ba to make this journey.

The akh was the form in which the deceased lived in the underworld, and was the union of his ka and ba. Once the akh had been created by this union, it survived as an 'enlightened spirit', enduring and unchanged for eternity.

▶ The ka of Awibra Hor
This ka statue came from a wooden shrine in the tomb of Hor, who ruled at Dahshur during the Thirteenth Dynasty (1795–1650 BC). The ka sign of a pair of raised arms is worn as a headdress. The statue, which is 1.70m (5ft 7in) tall, is the only known depiction of a ka as a three-dimensional sculpture.

The inlaid eyes give the statue a lifelike appearance.

The curved beard shows that the ka, like the king after his death, is identified with a god.

A heavy wig covers the head of the ka figure.

The plaster covering the statue cracked and came apart when it was unearthed.

▲ A bird with a human head
The word 'ba' has the same hieroglyph as the Jabiru stork. Migratory birds were regarded as incarnations of the ba, which could fly between the tomb and the underworld, so the ba is often depicted as a bird with a human head and, sometimes, human arms.

◀ The ba
Humans were not alone in possessing a ba. The gods also had their own, and the apis bull, for example, was the ba of Osiris. The ba was regarded by the Egyptians as a 'physical being', rather than a 'spirit', and as such had its own needs, including food, drink and sex.

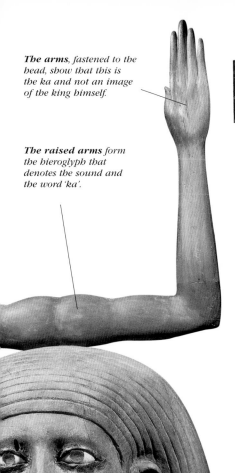

The arms, fastened to the head, show that this is the ka and not an image of the king himself.

The raised arms form the hieroglyph that denotes the sound and the word 'ka'.

INSIGHT

The statue – substitute for the body

For the Egyptians, the body was an essential element for the survival of the individual in the afterlife. This is why it was mummified and placed in an underground tomb for protection from grave robbers. Despite these precautions, it was not certain that the body could be preserved for ever. The Egyptians, therefore, sculpted statues of the deceased, ready to replace the body if it were to disappear.

The statue could then support the deceased's invisible elements, such as the ka. The ka could be invested in the statue and continue to live on the food offerings made at the tomb, and to sustain the deceased in the afterlife. In the tombs of the Old Kingdom, a windowless room, the serdab (Arabic for 'cellar'), was reserved for the statue of the deceased.

The statue of king Djoser (2667–2648 BC) seen at right came from a serdab near his pyramid at Saqqara.

◀ The akh
The spirit or the 'blessed' deceased, the akh is written with the hieroglyph of the crested ibis. This sign was also used to denote the words 'useful', 'profitable', 'efficient' and 'to shine'. Joined to the ka and the ba, the akh re-created the personality of the individual in the afterlife and ensured his survival throughout eternity.

Funerary Masks

Since the early mummification process was not a reliable one, the Ancient Egyptians covered the face of the deceased with a funerary mask that symbolically preserved the person's features.

The first examples of mummification date to the Old Kingdom (2686–2181 BC), when the the body was simply eviscerated, cleaned and wrapped first in bandages, then a shroud. In some cases, the linen bandages around the head were covered with a thin coat of plaster to emphasize the facial features, and the eyes, eyebrows and mouth were coloured with ink.

From the First Intermediate period (2181–2055 BC), the head was covered with a mask, usually made of inexpensive materials such as wood or cartonnage – layers of linen or papyrus stiffened with plaster. During the New Kingdom (1550–1069 BC) metal masks, hammered out of gold leaf, began to appear. For the pharaoh, his family and certain high-ranking officials, intricately worked gold plate was used, often inlaid with great quantities of glass and semi-precious stones. The deceased was believed to benefit from the precious metal, which symbolized the incorruptible flesh of the gods.

▼ The mask of Yuya
This mask of Amenhotep III's father-in-law, Yuya (c. 1390–1352 BC), found in his tomb in the Valley of the Kings, is a rare example of a gilded mask made for the mummy of a commoner.

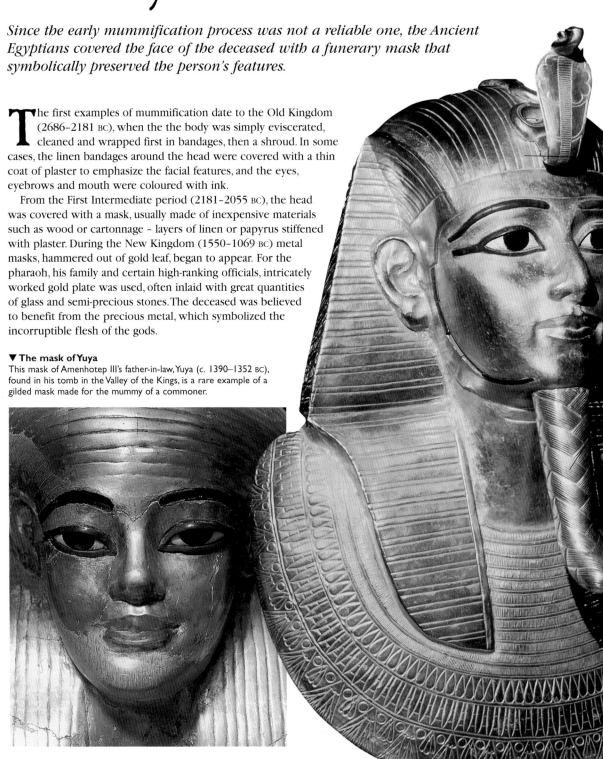

◄ Psusennes I

The funerary masks of the pharaohs were usually made from pure gold, such as this one of Psusennes I (1039–991 BC), or at least of wood covered with gold leaf. There are other characteristics: the head was covered with the nemes, the royal headcloth, and the face sported a long, rolled beard. The uraeus, the most important symbol of royalty, was set on the forehead. The masks were supported on a wide, bejewelled shoulder collar.

Psusennes I's mask is made from heavy gold, representing the 'flesh of the gods'.

The eyelids and eyebrows are coloured blue; a reference to the hair of the gods, which is usually represented by lapis lazuli.

The plaited beard, slightly turned up at the end, is symbolic of the divinity of the dead king.

▼ Egyptian and Greco-Roman elements

This funerary mask is made from gilded stucco on cartonnage. While the sides of the wig show traditional Ancient Egyptian motifs, the pink garland over the forehead is a Roman innovation.

◄ Mask from the Fayum

After a break of some 200 years, many masks were made in the Ptolemaic period (332–30 BC). Although they shared the same kinds of features as the earlier masks, their styling was very different. Particularly striking are the luminous colours of the winged sunrays over the brow, the uraeus and the striped design of the headcloth.

DOCUMENT

The gold mask of Tutankhamun

The funerary mask of Tutankhamun (1336–1327 BC), the child king from the Eighteenth Dynasty, was discovered in 1922 by Howard Carter. It is made from pure gold and inlaid with coloured glass and semi-precious stones. Apart from the nemes and the curved beard, the mask shows the uraeus and the vulture's head, symbolizing both halves of a unified Egypt, above its forehead. The royal robes have a broad shoulder collar inlaid with lapis lazuli, quartz, green feldspar, obsidian and glass. Whether or not the idealized features resemble those of the boy king is not known. The mask is on display at the Egyptian Museum in Cairo.

◄ The Middle Kingdom
The oldest plaster or cartonnage masks with multicoloured decorations come from the First Intermediate period, but they were common in the Middle Kingdom as well. This mask belonged to an Egyptian commander in Nubia. As in later times, the mummy masks from the Middle Kingdom had an extended breastplate, on which a broad pearl-encrusted collar was pictured.

The eyes are inlaid with white quartz and black obsidian; the eyelids and eyebrows are edged with blue glass.

▼ The Second Intermediate period
This mask from the Second Intermediate period (1650–1550 BC) shows the essential elements used in mummy masks until the Roman period – the striped headcloth and the broad shoulder collar with a row of red, blue and green pearls.

The first true mummy masks completely covered the head and upper part of the chest, and, although rare in the First Intermediate period, they were popular in the Middle Kingdom. Only the face, framed by a long wig, and the neck, adorned with a wide pearl necklace, were represented, while the rest was painted yellow or white.

At the end of the Middle Kingdom, bulkier masks appeared. Dainty faces formed a contrast to long, heavy wigs. Beneath the necklace, a column of text indicated the name of the deceased.

Changing styles

In the New Kingdom, masks were smaller and covered just the head and throat and occasionally the chest. Faces were less stylized, but they still possessed a long wig and a necklace of strings of pearls. In the Third Intermediate period (1069–747 BC) and the Late period (747–332 BC) funerary masks became increasingly small, until they covered only the head and neck.

By the Greco-Roman period (332 BC–AD 395), although Egyptian funerary customs remained popular, the overall shape and decoration of the mask had changed. The faces and headdresses had Egyptian gods painted on the sides, and the faces became more life like, forming actual portraits of the deceased.

Gold leaf covered the cartonnage to create the illusion of solid gold.

▶ King Amenemope
Found in a chamber originally occupied by the mummy of Mutnedjmet, one of Psusennes I's queens, at Tanis, the funerary equipment of the 21st-Dynasty king, Amenemope (993–984 BC), included a golden face mask and copies of his hands.

▼ Ptolemaic mask
In the Ptolemaic period (332–30 BC), traditional Egyptian design elements were mixed with Greek styles. The often gilded masks from this time show most of the traditional motifs.

▼ Roman times
Even after the Ptolemaic period, traditional elements such as the broad pearl collar remained, while some details, such as the golden earrings, were added.

The shoulder collar of Tuyu consists of several pearls, some of which are worked in the shape of flowers, inlaid with coloured glass.

▲ The mask of Tuyu
Tuyu was the mother of Tiy, the principal bride of Amenhotep III (1390–1352 BC). Together with her husband Yuya, she was buried – unusually for commoners – in the Valley of the Kings. The contents of the grave were discovered in 1905 and are now in the Egyptian Museum in Cairo.

The Mask of Tutankhamun

Of the spectacular treasures discovered in the famous tomb of Tutankhamun in the Valley of the Kings, his mummy mask, now displayed among the masterpieces of the Egyptian Museum in Cairo, is one of the most remarkable.

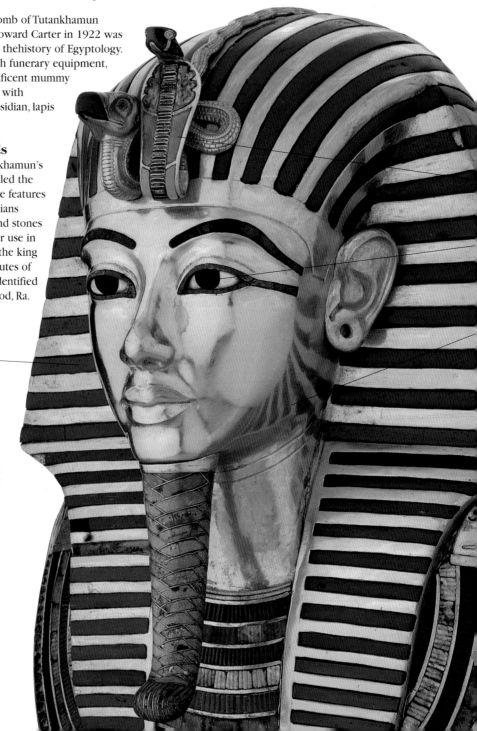

The discovery of the tomb of Tutankhamun (1336–1327 BC) by Howard Carter in 1922 was one of the greatest in the history of Egyptology. Among the young king's rich funerary equipment, Carter unearthed the magnificent mummy mask, made from solid gold with decorations in carnelian, obsidian, lapis lazuli and coloured glass.

The flesh of the gods

When Carter opened Tutankhamun's gold sarcophagus and revealed the mask, he saw a face with the features of a god. The Ancient Egyptians regarded precious metals and stones as divine materials, and their use in the funerary equipment of the king invested him with the attributes of a deity. Gold, for instance, identified the pharaoh with the sun god, Ra.

The nemes headdress is decorated with stripes of lapis lazuli, the blue of which contrasts with the bright yellow of the gold.

▶ **The attributes of the king**
Despite his association with the heretical reign of Akhenaten (1352–1336 BC), Tutankhamun is depicted here in the traditional regalia of the pharaohs. He wears the royal nemes headdress, striped with lapis lazuli and hanging down on either side of his face. The uraeus, or Wadjyt cobra, and the vulture goddess Nekhbet, symbols respectively of Lower and Upper Egypt, and of the king's sovereignty, sit side by side on his forehead, offering him their protection. His false beard, which identifies him with the gods, is worked in a framework of gold with blue glass paste inlaid to create a plaited effect.

▲ The pharaoh's eyes
Tutankhamun's expressive, almond-shaped eyes are emphasized and extended by eye make-up fashioned in lapis lazuli. The whites of the eyes are made from quartz, while the pupils have been inlaid with obsidian. A touch of red pigment has been added to the corner of the eyes to create a lifelike impression.

▶ The depiction of the king
Tutankhamun's parentage is uncertain – his father may have been Amenhotep III (1390–1352 BC) or, according to some Egyptologists, Akhenaten (1352–1336 BC). Although Tutankhamun is shown in the traditional, idealized manner of the pharaohs of Ancient Egypt, the influence of artistic styles popular during the reign of Akhenaten is evident. The facial features – notably the elongated oval of the face, the almond-shaped eyes, the long, slim nose and soft, full lips – are all typical of the Armana period's intimate, expressive portraiture. Tutankhamun's pleasant, youthful face is set in a serene, slightly sad expression.

The royal uraeus and Nekhbet vulture sit together on the pharaoh's forehead.

A realistic appearance was given to the eyes with the use of semi-precious stones.

The gold of the mummy mask identifies the pharaoh with the sun god, Ra.

The breast collar is comprised of 12 rows inlaid with lapis lazuli, quartz, turquoise and coloured glass.

▶ Rear view
The rear view reveals hieroglyphs inscribed on the king's back. These name the limbs of the deceased and identify them with a variety of deities, placing them under their protection. During the New Kingdom (1550–1069 BC), this formula came to be included in the *Book of the Dead*.

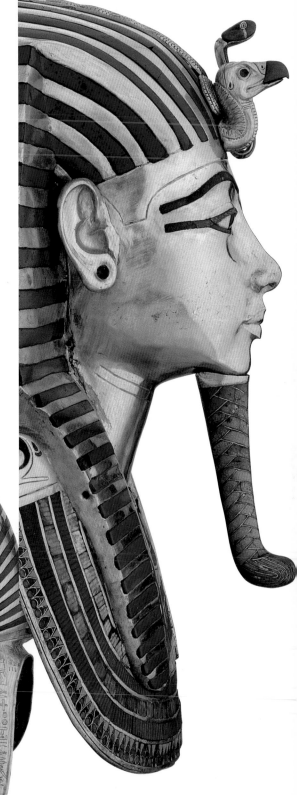

Rahotep and Nofret

Masterpieces of art under the Old Kingdom, the remarkably preserved statues of Rahotep and Nofret are among the finest and most lifelike works in the Egyptian Museum in Cairo.

S on of the pharaoh Sneferu (2613–2589 BC) and brother of Khufu (Cheops), Rahotep was a high priest of Ra at Heliopolis. His wife bore the simple title 'known by the king', which suggests that she was a lady-in-waiting. Their mastaba tomb at Meidum was discovered by the Egyptologist Auguste Mariette in 1871. Today, these remarkably well-preserved statues of painted limestone – with the colours still wonderfully bright and fresh – are major showpieces in the Egyptian Museum in Cairo. They are among the finest pieces of art from the early 4th Dynasty (2620–2500 BC).

The intact statues are so realistic that the workman who actually discovered them was terrified. He believed that he was in the presence of two living beings, who fixed their gaze on him in such a way that he felt, for a moment, rooted to the spot in their chamber.

INSIGHT

The Meidum necropolis

To the north of the pyramid of Sneferu at Meidum lie a number of painted tombs from the Fourth Dynasty (2620– 2500 BC). One of the most famous is the mastaba tomb of Rahotep and Nofret (below), in which their painted statues were found. A door relief from it is shown (right). Another tomb in the same cemetery contained the celebrated depiction of the Geese of Meidum.

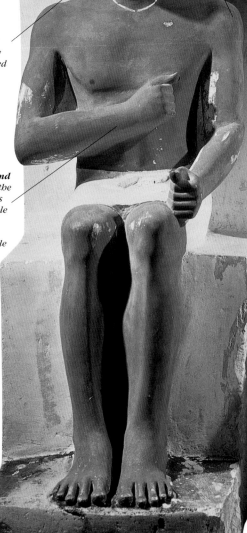

Men's skin was traditionally painted in red ochre.

The eyes, in rock crystal and white quartz, give the statue a lifelike appearance.

Rahotep's full mouth is highlighted by a black-painted moustache.

The right hand folded across the chest indicates Rahotep's noble status. The clenched fist represents male strength and dynamism.

The names and titles of the prince and his wife are inscribed on the high chairbacks. It is thought that they were the son and daughter-in-law of Sneferu.

Nofret wears a cloak over a tight tunic.

Nofret's open hand, in contrast to her husband's, indicates female passivity.

Women's skin was always painted in pale yellow ochre.

◄ **Nofret, a prince's wife?**
Nofret's sculpture is carved from a single block of limestone. The seat, with its backrest, is therefore an integral part of the piece. The statue of Nofret, 122cm (48in) high, is slightly taller than Rahotep's. She wears a heavy, shoulder-length wig, which is held in place by a headband decorated with floral motifs. Her own hair is flattened on her forehead. Nofret's rounded face is particularly attractive, with delicate features, full lips and large eyes. Around her neck is a throat-piece of alternating colours, ending in a row of pendants. Her white linen garments are close-fitting and reveal the form of her body.

◄ **Rahotep, the pharaoh's son**
With his short hair and fine moustache, Rahotep is a handsome man whose fine-featured face has been carved with great realism. He wears a short, white loincloth and, around his neck, a thin chain and pendant. Like Nofret, he is shown in the rather rigid pose with fixed gaze that was the conventional style of representation. The artist, however, has managed to imbue these statues with remarkable lifelike qualities. This is so that the deceased, who are represented in death by these effigies, can return to their bodies in the afterlife.

Royal Statuary

In the Egypt of the pharaohs, the most skilled sculptors were at the service of the king. In the royal workshops, they worked as teams, producing the statues that the kings ordered, chiefly for the temples dedicated to the gods and the ruler's funerary monuments.

From the Fourth Dynasty (2613–2494 BC), Egyptian art was created according to a set of rules which were to change little for 3,000 years. This is because art served a distinct purpose – it was not meant simply to depict an image, but also to bring that image to life. The statues in temples and tombs were designed to maintain an ideal world of health and happiness, free from the bad things in life. Death, decay and disease were rarely portrayed.

In the afterlife, a statue was intended to become the person it depicted. To this end, the opening of the mouth ceremony was performed on the finished work so that it could receive offerings of food and drink to sustain it.

It is not surprising, therefore, that the pharaoh, as the most powerful living human and god on earth, should commission hundreds of pictures and statues in his likeness. There were, of course, private statues that were placed in tombs, but nothing on the grand scale as that of the ruler.

◀ **Serene features**
The face of Khafra (2558–2532 BC), sculpted in alabaster, showed the ideal image of the monarch – calm and sure of himself, eternally young and strong, and the guarantor of cosmic order.

▶ **Amun and Tutankhamun**
The god Amun, here depicted with the features of Tutankhamun (1336–1327 BC), sits beside a standing figure of the king. Horemheb (1323–1295 BC), one of Tutankhamun's successors, commandeered the work by having his own names engraved upon it.

◀ **Menkaura and his wife**
The double statue of Menkaura (2532–2503 BC)
and his queen, tenderly holding her husband,
was among the first masterworks of royal
statuary. The shape of the faces and bodies,
the perfect polishing of the granite and the
simplicity of the composition are remarkable.

▼ **Rameses IV offering wine jars**
At the end of New Kingdom
(1550–1069 BC), the weakening of royal
authority affected the production of
royal statues. Fewer in number, they were
also less finished, as shown by this statue
of the pharaoh Rameses IV (1153–1147 BC)
bearing wine jars. Here the legs, in particular,
have been poorly finished.

Furniture for the Afterlife

Owing to the dry climate, many items from Ancient Egyptian tombs have survived, including wooden furniture and other objects made from transient materials.

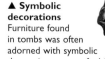

The tomb sites of settlement areas were not usually found to contain much furniture because the Ancient Egyptians generally reused their old furniture. Even so, most of our knowledge about the shape, use and construction of furniture, from the simplest to the most luxurious, is based on examples from tombs, or from tomb pictures showing daily life.

Wood – a precious material

Wood, particularly fine timber, was rare in Egypt and had to be imported from neighbouring countries. Especially prized was precious Lebanese cedar, which had to be transported by ship from Byblos. From tropical Africa, including the ancient land of Punt, came ebony, which was used for furniture and veneering.

▲ Symbolic decorations
Furniture found in tombs was often adorned with symbolic decorations, most of which related to permanence, regeneration and power. The ever newly born sun god was closely associated with the lion, seen here forming the graceful legs of this stool.

▶ Everyday furniture
This chair gives an example of the different materials and techniques used to construct furniture. The frame, back and legs are made from wood. The seat is woven from halfa grass or some other plant fibre.

◀ Relief from the tomb of Horemheb
This depiction of Horemheb (1323–1295 BC) comes from his first tomb in Memphis and shows the Eighteenth-Dynasty pharaoh sitting on an elegant chair. The slender legs, shaped like those of a predatory cat, are typical of this kind of upholstered chair favoured by the aristocracy, as are the struts.

▲ **Headrests**
A wooden headrest such as this one, combined with a pillow to make it more comfortable, was an essential item in the sleeping arrangements of most ordinary Ancient Egyptians.

▲ **Bed from Tutankhamun's tomb**
This comfortable wooden bed with its vertically panelled headrest, from the tomb of Tutankhamun (1336–1327 BC), has been overshadowed by more spectacular finds from the grave. The bed's surface is made from plant fibres woven in a pattern.

▼ **An elegant stand**
This wooden stand features a pot, in which a glass of water, beer or wine could be placed. Its surface has been painted with pretty motifs.

Ornate baskets were woven from reed, halfa grass and other plant fibres.

This small, painted wooden box was especially made for use in the tomb.

Smaller objects, as well as food items, were stored in baskets.

▲ **Decorations**
There were many ways to decorate a chair – different woods were used, or the chair might be inlaid or painted, with delicately woven seats.

Nefertari's Tomb

For his favourite wife Queen Nefertari (1300-1250 BC), the pharaoh Rameses II (1279-1213 BC) built the most beautiful tomb discovered in the Valley of the Queens.

The Italian Egyptologist Ernesto Schiaparelli (1856-1928) discovered the rock-cut tomb, or hypogeum, of Queen Nefertari in the Valley of the Queens in 1904. Built on the scale of a pharaoh's tomb, it is decorated with paintings of astonishing beauty.

As you enter the tomb from outside, a flight of steps leads into an antechamber decorated with images of the queen with various Egyptian gods. A vestibule and a side chamber lead off this main room. A second flight of stairs gives access to the burial chamber, which is supported by four pillars. On either side of the room are three chambers for tomb offerings, and the decorations retrace the journey of the queen into the afterlife .

Towards immortality

In the higher antechamber, the wall paintings show the queen being allowed access to the afterlife by the gods and being invested with magical powers. Only then can she make her descent into the burial chamber where, after passing through the gates to the underworld, she becomes like the god Osiris and possesses eternal life.

▶ **The vestibule**
Situated to the west of the antechamber, the vestibule has paintings of the queen being greeted by Neith (far right), before being led by the falcon-headed Horus towards the enthroned figures of Ra-Horakhty, the sun god, and Hathor, associated here with western Thebes. In her funerary aspect, Hathor was the goddess of the Theban necropolis and it was she who received the deceased into the underworld.

◀ **Valley of the Queens**
This desert valley, eroded by flowing water and wind, is one of the three Theban necropolises of the New Kingdom (1550–1069 BC). Mainly reserved for queens and princes, it contains about 80 tombs, most of them simply shafts. Of the 20 which are decorated, the most important is that of Nefertari.

Orientation of the tomb

Nefertari's tomb is built on a north–south axis, suggesting the course of the River Nile, whereas the journey of the deceased follows the sun from east to west. As she descends into the depths of the tomb, the queen is reborn, like Osiris.

Four pillars enclose the space reserved for the sarcophagus.

One of three small chambers in the burial chamber that held tomb offerings.

BURIAL CHAMBER

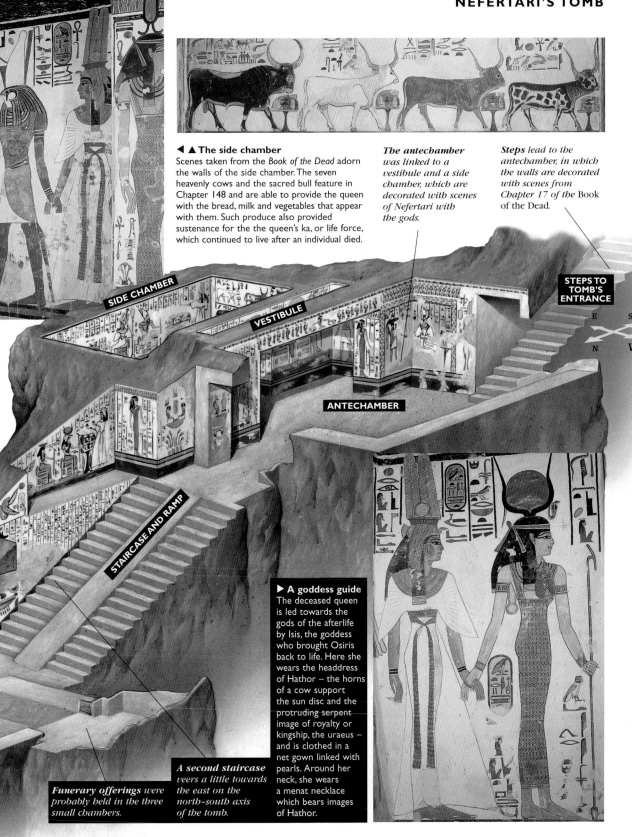

◀ ▲ The side chamber
Scenes taken from the *Book of the Dead* adorn the walls of the side chamber. The seven heavenly cows and the sacred bull feature in Chapter 148 and are able to provide the queen with the bread, milk and vegetables that appear with them. Such produce also provided sustenance for the the queen's ka, or life force, which continued to live after an individual died.

The antechamber was linked to a vestibule and a side chamber, which are decorated with scenes of Nefertari with the gods.

Steps lead to the antechamber, in which the walls are decorated with scenes from Chapter 17 of the Book of the Dead.

SIDE CHAMBER

VESTIBULE

STEPS TO TOMB'S ENTRANCE

ANTECHAMBER

STAIRCASE AND RAMP

E   S
N   W

▶ A goddess guide
The deceased queen is led towards the gods of the afterlife by Isis, the goddess who brought Osiris back to life. Here she wears the headdress of Hathor – the horns of a cow support the sun disc and the protruding serpent image of royalty or kingship, the uraeus – and is clothed in a net gown linked with pearls. Around her neck, she wears a menat necklace which bears images of Hathor.

A second staircase veers a little towards the east on the north-south axis of the tomb.

Funerary offerings were probably held in the three small chambers.

TREASURES OF THE AFTERLIFE

The tomb of Nefertari was restored between 1986 and 1992 by the Getty Conservation Institute, led by a team of specialist Italian restorers. Since the discovery of the tomb in 1904, the condition of the paintings had gradually deteriorated. The stone, and the layers of plaster which covered and supported it, had been attacked by salt, deposited on the walls by moisture. This included the water originally used to prepare the plaster and the paint, the Valley's infrequent but torrential rain that often flooded the tomb and the water vapour caused by the breath of visitors.

As a result, the paintings were beginning to 'lift' from the walls of the tomb. The restorers have mostly been able to halt the process of destruction, but the only way to protect the tomb further from the ravages of time has been to restrict the public's access to it.

▼ Pillar decorations
One of the four pillars in the burial chamber depicts Osiris and his son Horus. Wearing the leopard skin ritually worn by priests, Horus asks his father to judge Nefertari kindly.

The queen wears a vulture headdress surmounted by a sun disc and tall plumes.

Nefertari's gown is of thin pleated linen.

A wide decorative collar adorns the queen's neck.

Offerings to the gods

The walls by the staircase leading from the antechamber to the burial chamber are entirely decorated. On the upper part are depictions of Nefertari offering food and drink to the goddesses Hathor, Serket, Maat, Isis and Nephthys. Below are pictures of Anubis in the form of a crouching dog and the uraeus protecting the cartouche bearing the queen's name.

Geometric motifs *decorate the bracelets on the queen's wrists.*

Jars filled with wine *are offered to the gods.*

▲ Lost treasure
Several funerary items were found in Nefertari's tomb, one of which was this inlaid amulet of a djed pillar, said to represent the backbone, and thus the resurrection, of Osiris. The queen's tomb, looted since about 1100 BC, almost certainly contained many more riches.

▲ The queen's name
Like the body, the ba (soul), the ka (life force) and the shadow, the name was regarded as an essential element of every individual and had to be included in the deceased's tomb to ensure survival in the afterlife. Nefertari's name, enclosed in her royal cartouche, took the form of a statement: 'beloved of Mut'.

▼ Playing the game
This scene derived from the seventeenth chapter of the *Book of the Dead* shows Nefertari concentrating on a game in which she defeats her opponents in the underworld.

A Monumental Legacy

Colossal royal mausoleums and monuments to the gods are, and hold, ancient Egypt's most visible and tangible treasures. In their own time, these structures were symbols of authority and divine kingship. They were intended to impress Egypt's competitors and instill fear into her adversaries. Great tombs also aimed to smooth the kings' and upper classes' safe ride into the Afterlife, and ensured their place in history.

Four of the most potent symbols of Egypt, the Sphinx and the three pyramids of Giza, were built at breathtaking speed between 2589 to 2503 B.C.E. This has cemented the Fourth Dynasty in the first part of the Old Kingdom as one of the most visually impressive periods. It is hard to imagine that the 147-m (482-ft) tall Great Pyramid was built from five-ton limestone blocks in about 23 years.

There is another side to Ancient Egypt's monumental treasures – her vast urban sprawls. Made mostly of baked clay bricks on top of stone foundations, these cities' dwellings were packed tightly into narrow streets and quarters. But because of their fragile upper courses, evidence of many has been lost under the Nile's waters, or eroded and smothered by sand. However, there is enough to tell us that towns and cities were bustling and productive – with market places, artisans' quarters and stone temple areas.

The Great Pyramid
One of the seven wonders of the ancient world, the Great Pyramid was the tomb of Pharaoh Khufu. It was designed to surpass every previously built tomb and thus immortalize Khufu's reign. The king's family, government officials and household were buried in the surrounding necropolis.

Khufu, Builder of the Great Pyramid

Although Khufu, also known by his Greek name Cheops, was the builder of the first and largest of the three pyramids at Giza, little is known about his life and his only surviving image is a small ivory statuette excavated from a temple in Abydos.

Khufu (2589–2566 BC), the second pharaoh of the Fourth Dynasty, was the son of King Sneferu (2613–2589 BC) and Hetepheres (c. 2600 BC), a daughter of the last king of the Third Dynasty. Written documents show Khufu in a contradictory light. The Greek historians considered him a tyrant, but in Egypt he was generally looked upon as a wise and good king.

There is little information about Khufu's personality and his ways of government from contemporary sources, but it is evident that he fortified the kingdom founded

Kh

U

F

U

▲ **Khufu's seal**
The cartouche on the pharaoh's seal contains the hieroglyphs (above right) that spell his name. Khufu is the abbreviation of *Khnum-khuefui* – 'Khnum protects me'. Khnum was the ram god associated with the Nile floods and was one of the gods who created the universe.

▶ **Stone blocks**
The Great Pyramid at Giza consists of more than two million limestone blocks, each weighing at least 2.5 tonnes. In a building period of about 23 years, the length of Khufu's reign, one block would have to have been moved every five minutes to complete the work.

by his predecessors and increased the power of the state that they had carefully established.

A strictly organized administration ensured that the king's orders were followed, and that the resources of the state were well used. The key positions of government, as well as the highest priesthoods, were held by members of the king's household. Two of Khufu's sons, Djedefra (2566-2558 BC) and Khafra (2558-2532 BC), followed Khufu to the throne.

Prosperity and posterity

Neighbouring countries contributed considerably to Egypt's prosperity at this time. The badly needed wood for building purposes was imported from Lebanon. Sinai provided copper and valuable turquoise, and Nubia gold, while raids on Nubia and Libya yielded rich pickings in cattle and prisoners.

The Great Pyramid, with which Khufu immortalized his reign, was designed to surpass every tomb that had been built previously, and the king's family, household and government officials were buried in the surrounding necropolis. His mother, chief queens and other family are entombed in three smaller pyramids and mastaba tombs.

INSIGHT

Khufu's boat to the afterlife

In 1954, a boat, which supposedly took Khufu to the afterlife, was discovered on the southern side of the Great Pyramid. Separated into 1,224 individual pieces, it was found stowed in a cavity hewn out of rock and covered with stone slabs. After its removal, the boat was reconstructed over a period of years (below), and a museum was built on the spot where it was found. The boat is constructed of cedarwood, juniper and pine, and measures 43m (141ft) long and 5.9m (19ft 4in) wide.

Khufu – the second pharaoh of the Fourth Dynasty

The pharaoh's headdress is the red crown of Lower Egypt.

Khufu holds a flail, the symbol of his royal power, in his right hand.

Regal statues often show the ruler's left hand resting on his knee, as here.

Khufu's throne name appears in hieroglyphs on the right side of the throne.

The hieroglyphs in this cartouche are partially damaged.

The ivory statuette is only 7.5cm (3in) high.

▲ Khufu's image

The only remaining image of the builder of the Great Pyramid was found in the temple of Khentimentiu, in Abydos, and can now be seen in the Egyptian Museum, Cairo. The ivory statuette, only 7.5cm (3in) high, shows the enthroned king wearing the red crown of Lower Egypt. In his right hand he holds a flail, while his left hand is draped over his knee. On the throne, next to his legs, is his name.

▼ The final resting place

The tomb chamber of the pyramid of Khufu was built of red granite. The sarcophagus, made of the same material, was placed on the western wall during the building works. After the entombment of the ruler, the chamber was sealed with three stone slabs which served as trapdoors.

Building the Pyramids

At the beginning of the Old Kingdom around 2686 BC, the Egyptians invented a new form of royal tomb - the pyramid - and for more than 1,000 years kings were buried inside these imposing structures.

The first pyramid was built at Saqqara by the pharaoh Djoser (2667-2648 BC) and his architect Imhotep. It was also the first construction to be built in stone, rather than mud-brick. Djoser's pyramid seems initially to have taken the form of a mastaba, a rectangular tomb used for royal burials in the Early Dynastic period (3100-2686 BC). However, it was gradually modified and extended to become a pyramid-shaped structure consisting of six massive steps reaching a height of 60m (200ft). The steps represented the ladder, mentioned in the *Pyramid Texts* (funerary writings to help the deceased king attain eternal life), on which the king could climb to the sky. After unsuccessful attempts by two subsequent pharaohs to replicate the step pyramid, the pharaoh Sneferu (2613-2589 BC) abandoned this type of monument and built the first pyramid with sloping sides.

Planning ahead

Sneferu chose the site with care. It had to face west in accordance with the setting sun, be close to quarries for raw materials and have a rock foundation capable of supporting a massive quantity of stone. In addition, it needed to be out of reach of the Nile's annual flood. Work could commence only after the architect had completed his plan and calculated the amount of materials and men necessary for the construction. The ground also had to be levelled before astronomers fixed precisely the orientation of the pyramid's sides in relation to the cardinal points.

A funerary complex

The pyramid was just one part of a king's funerary complex. There was also a mortuary temple, where various rituals took place, and a causeway leading to the valley temple, where the pharaoh's body was received after its last journey along the Nile.

▼ The funeral procession
The deceased pharaoh's body was transported to the mortuary temple in a sacred boat made of wood. This was a scale model of an actual boat, and it was carried on poles by a slow-moving line of priests.

▶ Valley temple
Situated close to the port, the valley temple marked the entrance to the funerary complex. In one of the best preserved, the granite-built valley temple of Khafra (2558–2532 BC), there are two entrances which were probably protected by two pairs of sphinx separated by an obelisk. Inside, a vestibule led into a large, T-shaped room supported by pillars. Along the walls were statues of the pharaoh.
    According to some Egyptologists, the king's mummification may have taken place in the valley temple, or in a specially erected structure nearby.

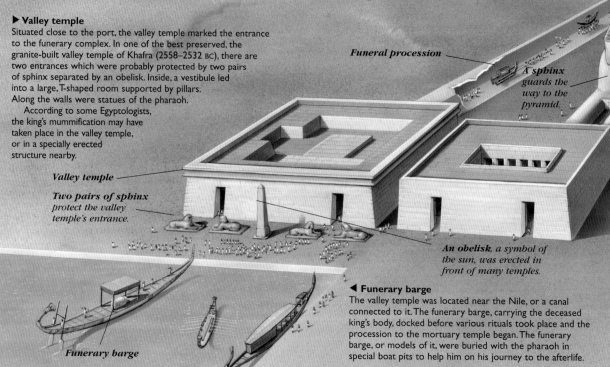

Funeral procession

A sphinx guards the way to the pyramid.

Valley temple

Two pairs of sphinx protect the valley temple's entrance.

An obelisk, a symbol of the sun, was erected in front of many temples.

Funerary barge

◀ Funerary barge
The valley temple was located near the Nile, or a canal connected to it. The funerary barge, carrying the deceased king's body, docked before various rituals took place and the procession to the mortuary temple began. The funerary barge, or models of it, were buried with the pharaoh in special boat pits to help him on his journey to the afterlife.

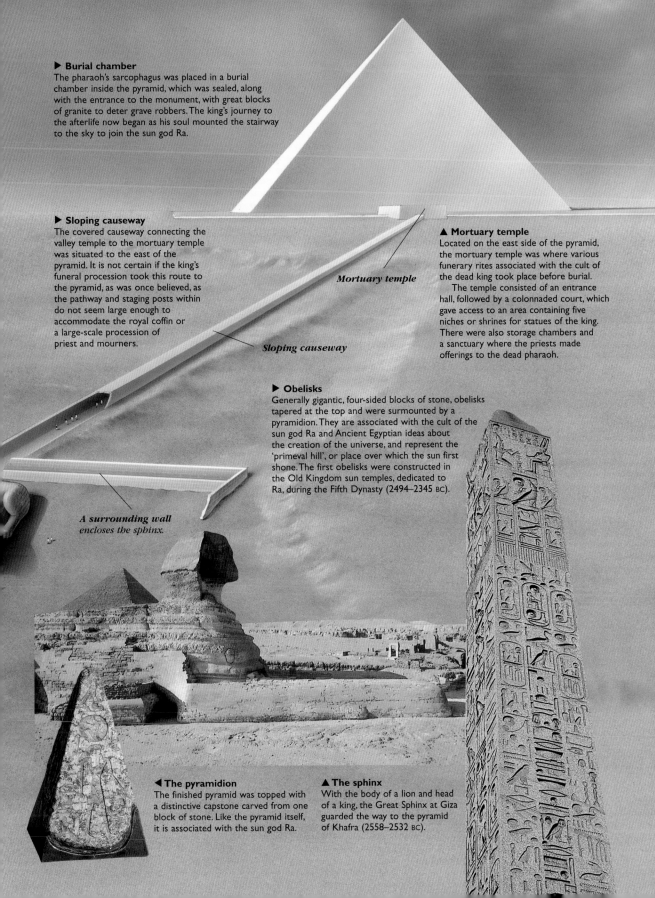

▶ Burial chamber
The pharaoh's sarcophagus was placed in a burial chamber inside the pyramid, which was sealed, along with the entrance to the monument, with great blocks of granite to deter grave robbers. The king's journey to the afterlife now began as his soul mounted the stairway to the sky to join the sun god Ra.

▶ Sloping causeway
The covered causeway connecting the valley temple to the mortuary temple was situated to the east of the pyramid. It is not certain if the king's funeral procession took this route to the pyramid, as was once believed, as the pathway and staging posts within do not seem large enough to accommodate the royal coffin or a large-scale procession of priest and mourners.

Mortuary temple

Sloping causeway

▲ Mortuary temple
Located on the east side of the pyramid, the mortuary temple was where various funerary rites associated with the cult of the dead king took place before burial.
The temple consisted of an entrance hall, followed by a colonnaded court, which gave access to an area containing five niches or shrines for statues of the king. There were also storage chambers and a sanctuary where the priests made offerings to the dead pharaoh.

▶ Obelisks
Generally gigantic, four-sided blocks of stone, obelisks tapered at the top and were surmounted by a pyramidion. They are associated with the cult of the sun god Ra and Ancient Egyptian ideas about the creation of the universe, and represent the 'primeval hill', or place over which the sun first shone. The first obelisks were constructed in the Old Kingdom sun temples, dedicated to Ra, during the Fifth Dynasty (2494–2345 BC).

A surrounding wall encloses the sphinx.

◀ The pyramidion
The finished pyramid was topped with a distinctive capstone carved from one block of stone. Like the pyramid itself, it is associated with the sun god Ra.

▲ The sphinx
With the body of a lion and head of a king, the Great Sphinx at Giza guarded the way to the pyramid of Khafra (2558–2532 BC).

Thebes, 'City of 100 Gates'

It was the Greek poet Homer (ninth or eighth century BC) who described Thebes as the 'city of 100 gates', in reference to the grandiose pylons that marked the entrances to the many temples and palaces built on both banks of the Nile.

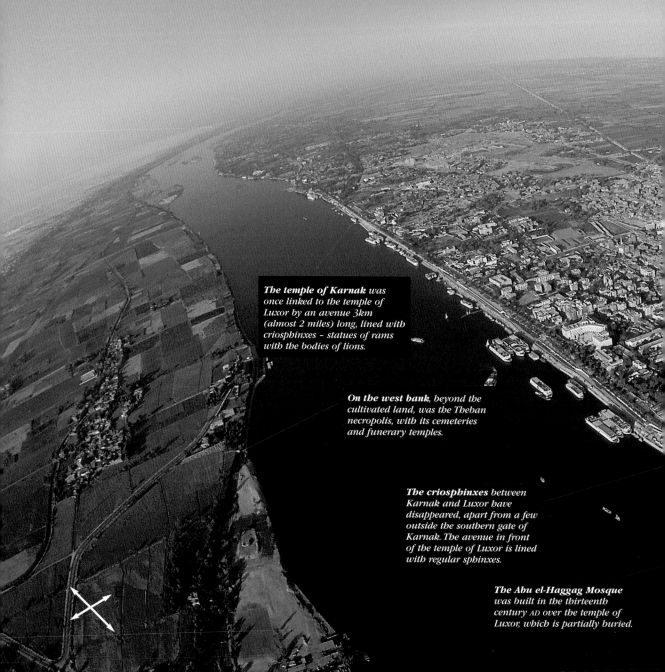

The temple of Karnak was once linked to the temple of Luxor by an avenue 3km (almost 2 miles) long, lined with criosphinxes – statues of rams with the bodies of lions.

On the west bank, beyond the cultivated land, was the Theban necropolis, with its cemeteries and funerary temples.

The criosphinxes between Karnak and Luxor have disappeared, apart from a few outside the southern gate of Karnak. The avenue in front of the temple of Luxor is lined with regular sphinxes.

The Abu el-Haggag Mosque was built in the thirteenth century AD over the temple of Luxor, which is partially buried.

◀ Ancient Waset

To the Ancient Egyptians, the town of Thebes was known as Waset, symbolized by the was sceptre adorned with a streamer and feather. It is written with the hieroglyph uas, symbol of power, the t sign for the feminine and the determiner for the city. It was also called niut, signifying the 'city' in the same way that Rome was designated simply by the word Urbs. It owes its name of Thebes to the Ancient Greeks.

▼ Thebes today

In only a few decades, tourism has transformed the small, sleepy town of Luxor into a rapidly expanding conurbation. Along its banks are dozens of boats which make cruises between the city and Aswan.

Thebes, once the capital of Ancient Egypt, has been built over by the present-day city of Luxor, the name of which derives from the Arabic 'el-Qusur', which describes the forts set up close to the temple at Luxor in Roman times.

A small, obscure town during the Old Kingdom (2686-2181 BC), Thebes was promoted to Egypt's capital after its princes had restored the unity of the country and founded the Eleventh Dynasty (2055-1985 BC). History repeated itself at the start of the New Kingdom (1550-1069 BC), when the Hyksos invaders were expelled and the country was unified under Ahmose.

During the New Kingdom, a succession of pharaohs enlarged and embellished the temple at Karnak, which was dedicated to Amun, Mut and Khons, as well as Montu, the local warrior god and protector of the city. The Luxor temple, situated a short distance to the south of Karnak, was founded by Amenhotep III (1390-1352 BC).

The Valley of the Kings on the west bank became the final resting place of the New Kingdom pharaohs, beginning with Thutmose I (1504-1492), and a long row of mortuary temples and royal palaces was built between the Theban hills and the River Nile.

The temple of Luxor has a majestic colonnade running parallel to the Nile.

East and west banks at Thebes

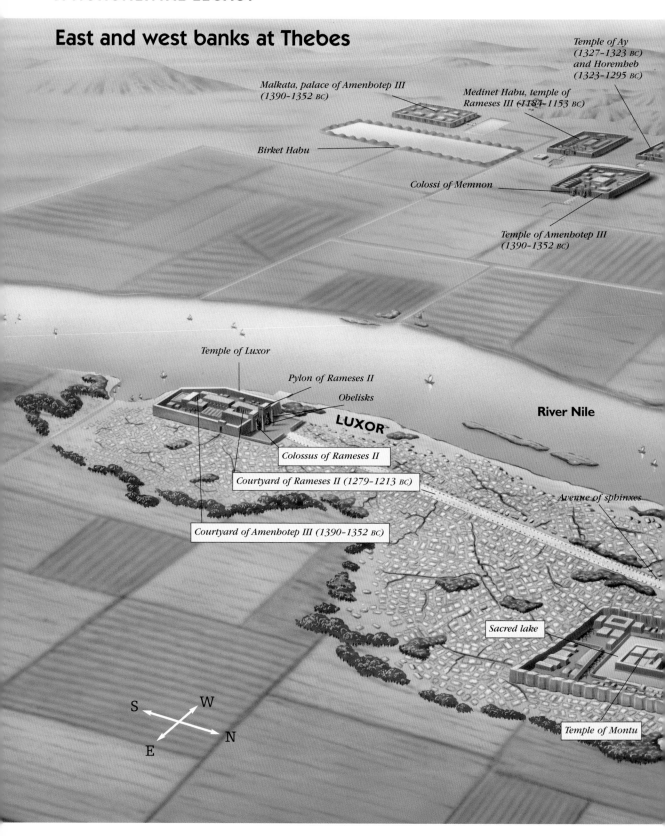

Temple of Ay
(1327–1323 BC)
and Horemheb
(1323–1295 BC)

Malkata, palace of Amenhotep III
(1390–1352 BC)

Medinet Habu, temple of
Rameses III (1184–1153 BC)

Birket Habu

Colossi of Memnon

Temple of Amenhotep III
(1390–1352 BC)

Temple of Luxor

Pylon of Rameses II

Obelisks

River Nile

LUXOR

Colossus of Rameses II

Courtyard of Rameses II (1279–1213 BC)

Avenue of sphinxes

Courtyard of Amenhotep III (1390–1352 BC)

Sacred lake

Temple of Montu

S W
E N

VALLEY OF THE QUEENS

Temple of Thutmose II
(1492–1479 BC)

Theban summit

VALLEY OF THE KINGS

Deir el-Medina:
workmen's village

Ramesseum, the funerary temple
of Rameses II (1279–1213 BC)

Temple of Mentuhotep II
(2055–2004 BC)

Temple of Thutmose III
(1479–1425 BC) at Deir
el-Bahri

Temple of Thutmose I
(1504–1492 BC)

Temple of Merenptah
(1213–1203 BC)

Temple of Saptah
(1194–1188 BC)

Temple of Thutmose III
(1479–1425 BC)

Temple of Tausret
(1188–1186 BC)

Temple of Thutmose IV
(1400–1390 BC)

Necropolis of Asasif

Temple of Hatshepsut
(1473–1458 BC) at
Deir el-Bahri

Temple of Amenhotep, son
of Hapu (1430–1350 BC)

Avenue of sphinxes

Avenue of criosphinxes

Landing stage

First pylon of Nectanebo I (380–362 BC)

KARNAK

Temple of Amun at Karnak

Temple of Khons

Sacred lake

Temple of Mut

Second
pylon

Third
pylon

Temple of Amun

A MONUMENTAL LEGACY

Western Thebes

For the Ancient Egyptians, the world of the dead was located to the west, where the sun disappeared in the evening before travelling through the underworld during the night. The Theban necropolis contained several cemeteries and funerary temples. The Valley of the Kings, first used by Thutmose I, houses the tombs of the pharaohs from the Eighteenth to the Twentieth dynasties.

Closer to the Nile, the Valley of the Queens contains the rock-cut graves of princes and royal wives, while the burial sites of nobles and high officials are concealed in the Theban hills facing the Nile river. The craftsmen who built and decorated the royal tombs lived at Deir el-Medina and had their own cemetery inside the village. Some monuments, such as the funerary complex of the pharaoh Mentuhotep II (2055–2004 BC) under the cliffs of Deir el-Bahri, date back to the Middle Kingdom (2055–1650 BC), when Thebes first became the capital of the country. The later funerary temples of Hatshepsut, Sety I, Rameses II and Rameses III are the best preserved on the west bank.

▲ Medinet Habu
The funerary temple of Rameses III (1184–1153 BC), stands at the southern end of the west bank, opposite modern Luxor.

▼ The terraced temple of Hatshepsut
Hatshepsut (1473–1458 BC) built her funerary temple on three levels under the cliffs of Deir el-Bahri, beside the earlier funerary complex of Mentuhotep II (2055–2004 BC).

▶ A narrow strip of land
The cultivable area on the west bank of the Nile at Thebes was flooded in ancient times by the annual inundation. It was bordered by the Theban hills, which contain hundreds of tombs.

▼ The Colossi of Memnon
These giant statues of Amenhotep III (1390–1352 BC) are the only remains of his funerary temple that began falling into ruin during the New Kingdom.

▶ The Ramesseum
In his funerary temple, with its massive pillars, or pylons, Rameses II (1279–1213 BC) recorded his military exploits at the Battle of Qadesh in Syria-Palestine.

Eastern Thebes

The living inhabited the east bank of the Nile in a collection of houses for ordinary people, residences for dignitaries and royal palaces. This is also the location of temples dedicated to several local gods. They were grouped around the temple of Amun, the head of the Ancient Egyptian pantheon, at Karnak.

Even when the administrative capital was moved to the Delta in the Eighteenth Dynasty (1550–1295 BC), Thebes remained the religious capital. As each king assumed power, he began a substantial construction programme in the temple of Amun, and the pharaohs continued to be buried in the Valley of the Kings.

◀ The criosphinxes
Statues of creatures with the body of a lion and the head of a ram, the sacred animal of Amun, protected the entrance to the temple of Karnak.

▶ The festival of Opet
Each year, Thebes celebrated the festival of Opet, during which the divinity of the pharaoh was renewed for the coming year in the temple of Luxor.

The ceremony began with a procession, on land or by river, carrying the statues of Amun, Mut and Khons from Karnak to Luxor, escorted by the king.

◀ The temple of Luxor
In contrast to Karnak, which was built over a period of 2,000 years, the temple of Luxor shows great unity. It was the work of only two kings – Amenhotep III (1390–1352 BC) and Rameses II (1279–1213 BC). Alexander the Great (332–323 BC) later added a sanctuary for the sacred boat of the god Amun.

▼ The temple of Karnak
The largest of all the temples of Egypt was dedicated to Amun, 'king of the gods'. It housed other temples, including one dedicated to his son Khons.

The Colossi of Memnon

Two mighty seated figures keep watch over the west bank of the Nile at Luxor. The colossi of Memnon are the guardians of the burial grounds which extend from the Valley of the Kings, past the mortuary temples of the pharaohs, to the Valley of the Queens.

Amenhotep III (1390–1352 BC), whose rule was marked by an extended period of prosperity and an extensive programme of new building, commissioned two gigantic seated figures to guard over the entrance of his mortuary temple, which today is completely destroyed. The pharaoh entrusted the task of building to his chief royal architect, Amenhotep, son of Hapu (c. 1430–1350 BC), who was later deified for his abilities and wisdom.

In his own image

The statues were made from single blocks of pink quartzite, each weighing more than 700 tonnes. The stone was quarried in the Red Mountain close to the old city of Heliopolis, near modern-day Cairo, and was transported several hundred kilometres to its final destination, using wooden sleds and barges for the journey along the River Nile.

Both statues portrayed Amenhotep III sitting on a throne in classic pose, with his hands resting on his knees and the cloth headdress, the nemes, on his head. The throne is engraved with the names and titles of the pharaoh, and images of protecting

The pharaoh carries the coiled cobra on his forehead to ward off his enemies.

The colossus wears the striped headcloth, the nemes, of the pharaoh.

This nineteenth-century illustration of the colossi shows the statues during the annual flooding of the Nile.

The pyramid-shaped mountain el-Qurn dominates the mountains of west Thebes at the Valley of the Kings.

The throne bears the pharaoh's name and title, and the symbols of the unification of Upper and Lower Egypt.

▼ Moving statues

In modern times, as in antiquity, the same methods have sometimes been used to move heavy objects. Giovanni Battista Belzoni (1778–1823), Egyptologist, engineer and exporter of Egyptian art, moved a gigantic figure of Rameses II in 1816. The seven-tonne bust was manually dragged to the banks of the Nile in the same way as it would have been thousands of years before. At first, no boats large enough to carry it could be found, and it took several months before one sturdy enough was available. The granite bust found its way to the British Museum in London in 1817.

PROFILE

'IMN

HTP

HQ'

W'ST

Amenhotep, lord of Thebes

Amenhotep III (1390–1352 BC)

The reign of Amenhotep III (below on his battle chariot) saw many changes in religion as he allied himself ever more strongly with the cult of the sun. Whether this was from religious conviction or simply a matter of politics is not known, but it certainly reduced the influence of then powerful priests of the god Amun.

Amenhotep III also elevated his own royal status, decreeing that he was not the son of the gods, but was himself a god, and that his monuments should be accordingly increased in grandeur. His cartouche bears his royal birth name Amenhotep, ruler of Thebes (right).

▼ Drawing history
Artists taking part in expeditions to Egypt in the eighteenth and nineteenth centuries produced accurate images of Ancient Egyptian monuments and artefacts in their sketches and drawings. Their efforts have ensured that, today, ancient monuments which have been damaged, either by vandalism or by construction projects, or which have completely disappeared, can be accurately reconstructed.

Mutemwiya, Amenhotep III's mother, is shown in a small statute to the right of the pharaoh's legs.

Tiy (c. 1410-1340 BC), the principal wife of Amenhotep III, is commemorated in a statue to the left of the pharaoh's legs.

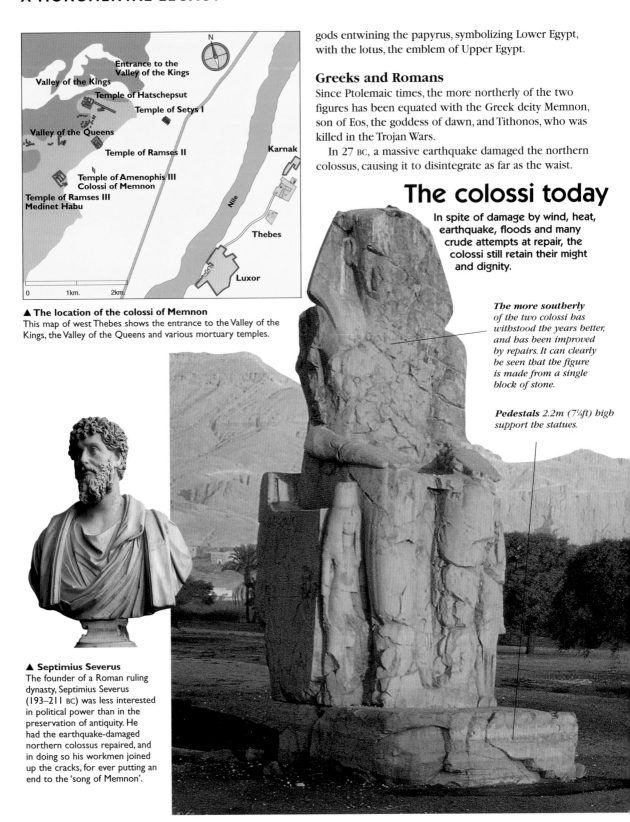

▲ The location of the colossi of Memnon
This map of west Thebes shows the entrance to the Valley of the Kings, the Valley of the Queens and various mortuary temples.

gods entwining the papyrus, symbolizing Lower Egypt, with the lotus, the emblem of Upper Egypt.

Greeks and Romans

Since Ptolemaic times, the more northerly of the two figures has been equated with the Greek deity Memnon, son of Eos, the goddess of dawn, and Tithonos, who was killed in the Trojan Wars.

In 27 BC, a massive earthquake damaged the northern colossus, causing it to disintegrate as far as the waist.

The colossi today

In spite of damage by wind, heat, earthquake, floods and many crude attempts at repair, the colossi still retain their might and dignity.

The more southerly of the two colossi has withstood the years better, and has been improved by repairs. It can clearly be seen that the figure is made from a single block of stone.

Pedestals 2.2m (7¼ft) high support the statues.

▲ Septimius Severus
The founder of a Roman ruling dynasty, Septimius Severus (193–211 BC) was less interested in political power than in the preservation of antiquity. He had the earthquake-damaged northern colossus repaired, and in doing so his workmen joined up the cracks, for ever putting an end to the 'song of Memnon'.

Soon after, the statue began emitting a musical note each morning. This 'singing' was interpreted as Memnon's greeting to his mother, the dawn, and people flocked from all over the ancient world in order to witness the phenomenon.

In reality, it appears that the morning sun heated the humid night air that was trapped in the cracks in the stone, and as the air expanded and was released, it created the musical note. When the Roman emperor Septimius Serverus had the statue restored in the third century AD, the statue sang no more.

▲ Reconstruction of mortuary temple's layout
From a few remaining paths and tracks under the orchards and fields, it has been possible to reconstruct the outline of Amenhotep's mortuary temple.

After earthquake damage in 27 BC, the northern colossus enchanted visitors with its 'singing', when warming air at dawn expanded and was pushed out through the cracks in the figure. The Roman emperor Septimius Severus supervised its restoration in the third century AD.

Originally 21m (69ft) high, including the now missing royal crown, the colossi today measure 19m (62ft).

The feet of the statues are nearly 3m (10ft) long.

Names of visitors, including the Roman emperor Hadrian, have been carved in the stone of the statues.

Flooding no longer threatens the colossi since the building of the Aswan High Dam.

Retaining wall

N

Sanctuary with pillared entrance

Third pylon

Second pylon   First pylon

Colossi of Memnon

▲ Emperor Hadrian
A lover of ancient cultures, the Roman emperor Hadrian (AD 117–138) visited the Memnon colossi in AD 130 during his travels through Egypt. Like many visitors before him, Hadrian could not resist the temptation to see his name carved on the base of one of the statues. The court poetess, who accompanied the emperor's party, also covered the legs with lines of verse.

Coptic, the Script of the Christians

Coptic was used in Egypt between the end of the Roman period (c. AD 395) and the Arab conquest (c. AD 641), and still survives in the religious services of the country's Christians.

The Egyptian language underwent a great deal of change in its 4,000-year history. For most of the pharaonic era, hieroglyphs were used, with hieratic as their cursive form. By the Twenty-Sixth Dynasty (664–525 BC), demotic replaced hieratic in commercial and bureaucratic documents, and by the Ptolemaic period (332–30 BC) it appeared on stelae such as the Rosetta Stone. Finally, during Egypt's Christian phase, Coptic script developed.

A Greek and Egyptian script

Christianity in Egypt emerged in the form of monastic communities, often in desert regions, and this characteristic gave rise to a need for written communication – for example, translating the Bible and conducting business affairs. Hieroglyphs could not be used as they were symbols of paganism, based on the same principles that had been employed to represent the old heathen gods and goddesses. The new church, therefore, adopted the Greek alphabet, with the addition of six letters derived from demotic to allow the transcription of intrinsically Egyptian sounds, and thus created the Coptic script.

▼ **The end of paganism**
The advent of Christianity meant the death of the Ancient Egyptian pantheon. In AD 535, the Byzantine emperor Justinian I sent soldiers to the temple of Isis at Philae, the last refuge of the old religion, to convert it into a Christian church.

▲ The monastery of St Anthony
Although Islam is the state religion, there are still Coptic communities in Egypt. The Monastery of St Anthony is one of the oldest in the country, and the monks here observe rituals that have remained largely unchanged for 16 centuries.

◄ A funerary stele
The distinctive Coptic cross dominates the surface of this funerary stele. Above it, a short inscription reads 'no one in the world is immortal'.

▼ Coptic dialects
Coptic was not a single, unified language, but was made up of at least six dialects. The most common form was Sahidic, which originated in Upper Egypt.

The jackal-headed god Anubis leads the deceased to Osiris, the god of the underworld.

A short inscription in Coptic lists the name of the deceased and the date of his death.

◄ The survival of ancient beliefs
At the beginning of the Coptic period (c. AD 395–AD 641), before most of the ancient temples had been closed by Theodosius the Great (AD 379–395), new Christian beliefs existed alongside the old religion of Egypt. This stele shows the gods Anubis and Osiris greeting the deceased in the underworld, yet features an inscription in the Christian language of Coptic.

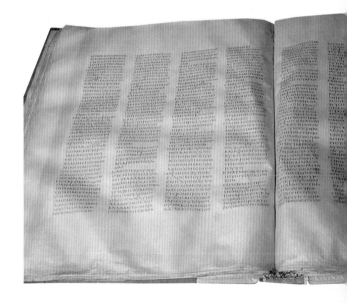

THE COPTIC ALPHABET

LETTER	NAME	PHONETIC VALUE	LETTER	NAME	PHONETIC VALUE	LETTER	NAME	PHONETIC VALUE
Ⲁ	alpha	*a*	ⲗ	lambda	*l*	Ⲯ	phi	*ph*
Ⲃ	beta	*b*	ⲩ	mu	*m*	Ⲭ	chi	*ch*
Ⲅ	gamma	*g*	Ⲛ	nu	*n*	Ⲯ	psi	*ps*
Ⲇ	delta	*d*	Ⳉ	xi	*ks, x*	ⲱ	omega	*o*
Ⲉ	epsilon	*e*	Ⲟ	omicron	*o*	ⲱ	shaj	*sch*
Ⲍ	zeta	*z*	Ⲡ	pi	*p*	Ϥ	faj	*f*
Ⲏ	eta	*e*	Ⲣ	rho	*r*	Ϩ	hori	*h, ch*
Ⲑ	theta	*th*	Ⲥ	samma	*s*	Ϫ	dshandsha	*tsch*
Ⲓ	iota	*i, j*	Ⲧ	tau	*t*	Ϭ	shima	*c, kj*
Ⲕ	kappa	*k*	Ⲩ	upsilon	*u, w, y*	Ϯ	dij	*ti*

Peacocks, Christian symbols of eternal life, appear at the top of the stele.

A depiction of a Christian chapel dominates the stele's surface.

► **The stele of Sabek**
This richly decorated funerary stele from Upper Egypt provides an example of the type of abstract design that was a feature of Coptic art. Beneath the image of a chapel, framed by peacocks and interlaced patterns, is an inscription which gives the name of the deceased and the date of his death, as well as a short prayer.

◄ **Information about the deceased**
The inscriptions on Coptic funerary stele are characteristically very short. On this stele from the eighth century AD, just the name of the deceased appears, above a stylized depiction of a building.

Coptic was comprised of a series of dialects, of which at least six had the status of written language. The most important were Sahidic, which originated in Upper Egypt; Bohairic, spoken in the Delta region; and Fayyumic, the version found in the Fayum and its environs. Of these, it was Sahidic that developed into the standard form of the language.

Coptic in Christian services

The Arab conquest of Egypt in the seventh century AD signalled the demise of the Coptic language. The Christian script was pushed aside in favour of Arabic, the tongue of the new Islamic rulers. By the seventeenth century, Coptic had ceased to be spoken even in the most remote villages of Upper Egypt.

However, as late as 1936, the Coptic specialist Werner Vycichl found people living near Luxor who claimed to speak the language within the family. It also still exists in certain parts of the Coptic Christian service, although much of this has been translated into Arabic. Furthermore, Jean-François Champollion's knowledge of Coptic was a key factor in enabling him to decipher the hieroglyphs of the Rosetta Stone and unlock the mysteries of the ancient language of the pharaohs.

A short prayer has been inscribed, as well as the deceased's name and the date of his death.

▼ Writing utensils
Scribes in the Coptic period used equipment similar to that of their pharaonic counterparts. Their reed pens and inkwells were kept in leather cases such as this one, which bears an image of St George.

◄ The monasteries
Christianity in Egypt began life in the form of monastic communities established in the wilderness of the country's desert landscape. Monasteries such as St Anthony's and St Paul's were founded by early Christians who had fled from religious persecution at the hands of the Roman rulers. The monks were instrumental in the development of the Coptic script – a means of written communication without the taint of paganism inherent in hieroglyphs.

The Fayum Portraits

The Fayum Portraits, discovered by Flinders Petrie in the late nineteenth century, are striking depictions of members of the elite in Greco-Roman Egypt and combine Classical styles of art with Ancient Egyptian funerary traditions.

During the Greco-Roman Period (332 BC–AD 395), traditional Egyptian funerary practices and artistic styles came under the influence of Classical models. This is powerfully illustrated by the Fayum Portraits, a collection of mummy masks discovered by the celebrated British Egyptologist Flinders Petrie, at Hawara in the Fayum region in 1888. They were painted in encaustic, a technique that employs a mixture of wax and pigment, creating vivid colours that enhance the strikingly naturalistic depictions of the portraits' subjects.

Images from life

The portraits depict elite members of the Greco-Roman community in Egypt, often in their finest clothes and jewellery, in their prime, or even in their youth. Painted on thin wooden panels, they show their subjects with realistic facial features and an intense, expressive gaze.

▼ The Fayum Oasis
The Fayum Portraits take their name from the Fayum Oasis, where they were discovered by Flinders Petrie in the late nineteenth century. This fertile region in Egypt's Western Desert was an important economic and cultural centre from the Middle Kingdom (2055–1650 BC).

Items of jewellery such as these earrings have been instrumental in the dating of the portraits.

The encaustic technique, which employed a heated mixture of wax and pigment, was used to great effect.

◀ Depictions of women

The portraits of women have a delicacy and detail that is absent from those of their male counterparts. A considerable degree of attention is paid to hairstyles and items of jewellery. The necklaces, brooches and earrings that the women are pictured wearing have provided a catalogue of jewellery of the Roman period in Egypt (30 BC–AD 395). In addition, they have helped Egyptologists to date the portraits accurately.

▶ Mummy portrait of a man

This painted and gilded stucco mummy case from the Fayum Oasis dates from the early first century AD and illustrates the combination of Classical and Egyptian styles present in the Fayum Portraits. Traditional Egyptian funerary scenes appear beneath an image of the deceased's face.

Golden motifs have been attached to the bright red cloth wrapped around the mummy.

Typical Ancient Egyptian funerary images decorate the mummy, including a goddess with her arms spread protectively.

◀ A distinguished portrait

As indicated by the bald head and full beard, this portrait depicts a man in middle age. He is dressed in a tunic decorated with pink bands featuring a geometric motif on the shoulders and regards the observer with a direct, dignified gaze.

The style of the man's beard is one of the elements that has helped historians to date the portrait.

This portrait from the Fayum region has been dated to the second half of the third century AD.

A MONUMENTAL LEGACY

Painting techniques

Numerous examples of this type of portrait have been discovered in Egypt, in sites as diverse as Saqqara and Aswan, as well as at Hawara in the Fayum region. Earlier pieces were executed in encaustic, but later ones, particularly those dating from the fourth century AD, were painted in tempera – a technique that blended pigment with water and an adhesive material, usually egg white. These watercolour portaits are sadly not as well preserved as their sturdier, wax-based counterparts.

Funerary traditions

The extent and detail of individual characterization seen in the Fayum Portraits led Flinders Petrie to believe that they were painted in the owner's lifetime and were intended to be hung in their home until their death. It appears, however, that after the second century AD most of the portraits were painted after the death of the subject. They were placed over the face of the deceased's mummified body by enclosing the edges of the mask in the outer layers of bandages.

The Fayum Portraits are truly original pieces of art, representing a synthesis of the naturalistic Classical style of portraiture with the Ancient Egyptian concept of death as a gateway to a continuing existence in the afterlife. The portraits have provided Egyptologists with a wealth of information regarding high-status members of Greco-Roman society in Egypt – in particular their clothing, adornment and physical characteristics – as well as being masterpieces of art in their own right. Now mostly detached from their mummies, some of the finest examples are on display in the Egyptian Museum in Cairo and the Petrie Museum in London.

Executed in encaustic, this portrait has been painted directly onto a piece of cloth rather than wood.

The high status of the individual depicted here is indicated by his fine clothes and jewellery.

▼ **The sign of life**
The portrait of Ammonios features the ankh sign, the Ancient Egyptian hieroglyph denoting life. The ankh was eventually adopted by the Coptic church and remains its unique form of the Christian cross, known as the *crux ansata.*

◄ **Roman portraiture**
This Ancient Roman double portrait serves as an illustration of the extent of Roman influence on art in Egypt during the period of Roman rule. The naturalistic depiction of facial features, direct gaze of the subjects and use of light and shade all bear a distinct similarity to the artistic techniques used in the Fayum Portraits. This painting of Terentius Neo and his wife was found among the ruins of their house in Pompeii.

THE FAYUM PORTRAITS

◄ Portrait of Ammonios
This portrait, painted in the encaustic technique on canvas, was discovered in the Roman town of Antinoopolis in Middle Egypt. It depicts an elegantly dressed young man holding a vessel of wine in his right hand and a small bouquet of roses in his left hand. Above his shoulders are the ankh sign and an amulet figurine.

▲ A floral motif
The rose had a symbolic meaning for the Ancient Romans. It was regarded as a symbol of perfection, and Roman emperors sometimes wore wreaths of the flower as crowns.

▼ A golden goblet
The double-handled goblet shown in Ammonios's right hand resembles the communion cups, such as the one shown below, used in the Christian church.

▲ Portrait of a lady

Painted on a background of cedar wood, this portrait comes from Antinoopolis in Middle Egypt and dates from around AD 120. It shows a young woman, with fair, delicate skin, swept-back hair and large, dark eyes. The mantle she wears has been delicately fashioned in gold leaf.

▲ ▶ Roman fashions

This funerary stele (top right) shows a woman wearing the same type of hairstyle as that of the woman in the portrait above. The deceased also wears a piece of typically Roman jewellery in the form of a large collar around her neck.

▶ A likeness in tempera

This portrait from the first century AD has been executed in tempera as opposed to the usual encaustic. The tempera technique, which involves mixing pigments with a water-soluble binding agent rather than wax, has the effect of creating strong, translucent colours. When Italian Egyptologist Ippolito Rosellini (1800–1843) saw the portrait, he was struck by its resemblance to his own mother.

INSIGHT

An ongoing tradition

The custom of depicting the face of the deceased on their mummies remained an element of Egyptian funerary tradition until the end of the fourth century AD. Some of the Fayum Portraits include decoration delicately worked in gold leaf, a feature of numerous mosaics of the Byzantine period.

A number of other characteristics of the Fayum Portraits are found in paintings of individuals in later epochs. The intense, direct expression delivered by large, dark eyes, the naturalistic features and the use of light and shade are all present in Western portraiture over the centuries. The Fayum Portraits are the earliest such works of art and their poignancy makes them truly enduring masterpieces.

▲ Found in the Fayum region, this portrait is painted in encaustic on wood and dates from the second century AD.

▲ This mosaic from the Byzantine church of San Vitale in Ravenna in Italy depicts the Empress Theodora.

◀ The long face and large eyes in this painting by the seventeenth-century artist El Greco recall the Fayum Portraits.

◀ The elongated proportions seen in early twentieth-century painter Amedeo Modigliani's work create a powerful sense of melancholy similar to that present in some of the Fayum Portraits.